Michael Mish • Jennifer Schloming

Maya and the Gordian Knot

Unraveling the Mysterious Journey Through Grief

Copyright © 2011 Michael Mish and Jennifer Schloming
All Rights Reserved
ISBN 978-0-9848294-0-8

No part of this book may be reproduced in any form or by any electronic or mechanical means, including information storage and retrieval systems, scanning, electronic distribution without permission in writing from the publisher, except by reviewers who may quote brief passages in a review.

For information contact:
info@mgkpublishers.com

Michael Mish
PO Box 3477 • Ashland, OR 97520

Jennifer Schloming
3212 Pioneer Road • Medford, OR 97501

Book Quotes:

"Life is eternal, and love is..."
A Commendatory Prayer, Rossiter Worthington Raymond,
Bartlett's Familiar Quotations ©1968. John Bartlett.
Little, Brown and Company, New York, NY

"Time is a physician..."
Diphilus, 3rd cen. B.C., Greek

"Sorrow makes us all children..."
Ralph Waldo Emerson, Emerson in His Journals ©1982,
selected and edited by Joel Porte, Harvard University Press, Cambridge, MA

"When you are sorrowful look again..."
Kahlil Gibran, The Prophet ©1923, A.A. Knopf, New York, NY

"O Swear not by the moon, the fickle moon,..."
Shakespeare, *Romeo and Juliet, Act II, Sc. 2*, ©1955. Cambridge University Press, UK

"You left me boundaries of pain..."
Emily Dickinson, *Love, II*, Emily Dickinson, Complete Poems ©1924. Secker, London

"Good night, good night..."
Henry Wadsworth Longfellow, *Three Friends of Mine, IV*,
The poetical works of Henry Wadsworth Longfellow ©1891.
Houghton, Mifflin, Boston, MA

"We shall not cease..."
T.S. Eliot, *"Little Gidding,"* Collected Poems, 1909-1962 ©1963
Harcourt, Brace & World, New York, NY

"Eternity is really long..."
Woody Allen, Just Six Numbers ©2000, Martin Rees. Basic Books, New York, NY

Editor: Julia Sommer • Ashland, Oregon
Graphic Designer: Jim Marin • Jacksonville, Oregon

Dedication

For Galen, who has his own story and is the reason for mine. For Jim, who knows that this history precedes him and still loves me. Jim, who took our words and made them beautiful. For Peter, who brought his love and his wonderful dying son into our lives, and who gave space that I might write. For Julia, who edited with great care and genuine desire that our stories might come round right. To Jake, Chet, Spunky and Rosie, who have held the field around us and loved us unconditionally. Who carried our grief and still wagged and purred. And finally, for my family and friends who caught Galen and me when we were falling. To all of you, I offer my greatest gratitude.

— Jennifer

Life is eternal, and love is immortal,
and death is only a horizon;
and a horizon is nothing save the limit of our sight.

— Rossiter Worthington Raymond —

The Courage to Continue the Journey

To bring you into our lives, our stumbling confusion, our hopes, and our new convictions is an enormous privilege for us. In presuming on your attention as a reader, it is our hope that our work may leave you feeling kinder toward your own grieving and less willing to tolerate anyone else's judgment of what it should look like. Forgive yourself for what you don't already know, and be assured that there are at least two people who have faced the hash the world makes of itself in loss who hold you in their hearts.

The task of ongoingness is enormous. We honor your labor, your courage, and your hope to do it well, whatever that may look like. Blessings on your passage, on coming home whole again.

With love,

Michael and Jennifer

Time is a physician that heals every grief.

— Diphilus —

Table of Contents

INTRODUCTION
Enduring Together: *Intimate Inquiries in the Mirror of Grief* 1

SECTION ONE
Michael's Story: *Maya* 5

SECTION TWO
Jennifer's Story: *The Gordian Knot of Intimacy* 87

SECTION THREE
A Conversation: *Where We Are Today* 167

EPILOGUE
Somewhere This Side of Eternity: *Time* 187

*Sorrow makes us all children again -
destroys all differences of intellect.
The wisest know nothing.*

— Ralph Waldo Emerson —

Enduring Together
Intimate Inquiries Through the Mirror of Grief

On the choir director's recommendation, I took my 8 year old son, Galen, to audition for a man who had just written a musical and was having a hard time finding boys who could sing and act. Galen was interested, so I called about it. I explained that Galen's dad had just died and that any test he faced right now, including an audition for a stranger, needed to be offered with respect for how incomprehensibly vulnerable he was. There was no way of knowing how a stage experience would prove out—it might or might not be good medicine. After a brief pause, the man on the other end of the phone said, "I understand exactly. My wife died two months ago." And so, Michael and I met. Through the most alarmingly tenuous moments of our madness, we held one another's safety by phone. We would call one another for "sound checks." To know that we each still were, that the particular shape of this day's weirdness was recognizable to someone else, and that neither was cruising off some edge where no one could fish us back again. It is in this sense that we loved each other through the worst of it—by simply being there. Answering the phone and being; holding the fragments of our lives in Ma Bell's lines.

— Feb. 1995

Walking Together Under a Midnight Sky

We are a mid-life pair of friends who have survived within the embrace of one another's compassion, patience, and insight as we've each traversed the landscape of grief. Our spouses died within one month of each other, and we came new into one another's lives in the first few weeks after these losses. We have continued a deepening dialogue on the mystery and demands of surviving well—tending one another through the initial shattering to the greater grace that reaches toward a more ample personhood. We have abided with one another as we each have worked to live unafraid, more whole and with clearer purpose. We have struggled to claim the undiminished vitality that can be the gift of hard-reckoned loss.

Each isolated in our grief, Michael and I began talking together, filling the air with the sounds of our voices. Our conversations offered essential gravity to the bewilderment of those initial days, months, years. We held one another's silences as well. We have, in short, helped keep each other alive, and would like, through this book, to offer what we have learned about surviving well. Because we are friends rather than lovers, we offer two distinct points of view. We do not suffer the burden nor enjoy the blessing of an obligation to a third identity as a married couple.

If you were to ask whether we are doing this for our own healing, we would say that of course we are. It seems that suffering resolves into a greater wholeness when its lessons can help illumine the way for someone new. It is our hope in this book to befriend the reader's loss in ways that invite more generous patience, self-forgiveness, and finally, meaning.

The format of this book honors our separate voices and perspectives, mining the differences that gender and type of loss might offer. At the conclusion of the book, we own up more fully to our shared world as professional musicians. We look more closely at how we sense music shapes matter, both creates and moves us, and where it fits into our daily lives as the unnoticed medicine of body, heart, and soul.

It was 16 years ago that Michael and I excavated the ground of our own grief. This is our chronicle of the initial efforts to survive, as well as a backward glance from where we are now. We hope it will help reveal where breath is stolen by toxic particles of loss—the accumulated moments, both thunderous and silent, that flatten and diminish our wonder at being alive. We invite you to journey with us.

Jennifer Schloming
— June 2011

Like the nuclear "fleas," the microscopic bits of radiation being carried on the wind from Fukushima, we are all breathing grief on the inhale. Not just the obvious disappointments and losses, but the unnoticed filaments of despair that attach to our lungs and rob us of breath, vitality, hope, and life.

SECTION ONE

Michael's Story
Maya

*When you are sorrowful
look again in your heart, and you shall
see that in truth you are weeping for
that which has been your delight.*

— Kahlil Gibran —

Top: Our wedding ceremony in Assisi, Italy, August 1994. Bottom: Married for only a few weeks, in Aspen during John Denver's Windstar Symposium for which I was the children's music director.

Michael's Story: Maya

Clockwise from the top: Home marriage ceremony. Together in Lithia park, Ashland. After our marriage ceremony in Assisi, Italy August 1994. In our Ashland, Oregon home. Portland, May 1994 on our way up to a backpacking trip in the Olympic Peninsula, shown here with Sophie Gardner

Maya

Beginning of the End…
The Flight
Written January, 2001

"Do you hear that buzzing noise?"

She agreed that she did hear the buzzing. But she couldn't have. At least not this noise. My body was buzzing with the persistent ring of a factory alarm. I had no idea what was going on.

"You really do?" I persisted.

"Yes" she replied, with an almost annoying calm.

I wondered if she was just agreeing with me. I was, after all, interviewing her to be a second housemate. She sat with regal reserve in my kitchen near the wood stove's radiating warmth as the newly stoked fire snapped impertinently.

"My God, this woman looks like an angel," I thought to myself. Feeling the intensity of my eyes taking her in, her regality slipped into a self-consciousness that spoke of a restless, insecure child just beneath her controlled surface. She shifted her weight in the wooden kitchen chair and told me she was new here. She spoke of her new practice as a therapist, containing her excitement as she caught herself being swept up in the enthusiasm of her own words.

She looked like a flight attendant for a Swedish airline, professional and neat as a pin in pink and yellow. What kind of unearthly perfection had walked into my kitchen asking to live in my house?

It started again. The factory alarm was vibrating my body with a wasp-like insistence.

"Sorry, but you DO really hear that buzzing sound?"

She nodded.

In retrospect, it was my body sounding an alarm. An alarm letting me know that, in no uncertain terms, MY LIFE WAS ABOUT TO CHANGE BECAUSE OF THIS WOMAN.

I had no concern at the time about how my life might change. I was in rapture. I was thinking, "these are the sounds of love-at-first-sight—bells, music, violins, angel voices…uh, buzzing."

ND0>Dutifully I put aside, as best I could, my raging hormone response to this woman, and she moved in, but I had no intention of falling in love with a housemate. I would have strict boundaries on myself. It was to be clearly a monthly rent relationship. That was it. No ifs, ands, or buts.

Three months later in the late spring with the heady smell of lavender, grass, and honeysuckle in the air, I did something without precedent. I did something that surprised me. I did something that ran so completely at variance with the way I saw myself and the way others saw me. I asked her the following question:

"Maya, will you marry me?"

I could not believe I had uttered the words. They felt foreign. My mouth seemed to have taken leave from whatever relationship it had with my brain.

"OK…alright, don't answer right now…think about it. Let me know later," I said, dumbly.

My brain, as if with arms crossed and foot tapping, was now looking at my mouth with complete incredulity. I was parroting, verbatim, words from some Hollywood movie romance I must've seen as a kid. That wasn't me saying, "Don't answer….."

Maya went quiet. There was a long pause. She suggested that we speak about this later, and not on the phone. I agreed. I hung up the phone and began pacing around my bedroom in disbelief as to what I had just done. This was a life-changer. A pivotal moment in my life.

Driving back to Oregon from California, she told me she had given it a lot of thought. She said yes.

Yes!

And we set a date for mid-summer.

Drunk with new love's intoxicant, the months that followed found us discovering each other petal by petal. We were on our best behavior and all was right with the world. It was the end of winter and the beginning of spring. A window was flung open and a flood of sunlight and prismatic, gossamer-winged forms filled our house. The pinks and yellows she wore finally worked their magic, wooing spring out of its long winter sleep.

I looked so very forward to simply waking up in the morning so we could invent things to do together. And invent we did. We hiked. We backpacked. We traveled. We kept to ourselves, hardly socializing at all, as if to respectfully keep this delicate butterfly aloft and not poisoned by the reality of the day-to-day. She would coo the words that would melt me in some ancient place in my body:

"I'll be a good wife to you…"

I told her how eager I was to be her husband.

My body's buzzing was echoed by the buzzing of the bees as they careened about the rosemary bushes greedily overgrowing their borders outside the front door. Their buzz grew to a drone as spring slid promisingly into summer. In fact, all of nature sang in one supernal symphony of rebirth. Colors were intensely brighter. I was lighter. In a picture that a stranger took of us in our nearby park, we looked like two colorful flowers bending toward each other in a meadow.

Apart from the day she came home from the dentist after having a root canal, everything seemed nearly too perfect. Maya and our other housemate, Judith, finished a bottle of wine together and Maya's regal and calm exterior melted away. She became funny. Bawdy. Even a little messy. Until—she seemed like a different person. After the laughter had died down and Judith withdrew to her room, I followed Maya into her bedroom and asked if she'd ever had problems with alcohol. She sweetly, and with her infinitely serene sunflower of a face, assured me that it had been the dental anesthetic in combination with the wine that had made for her strong reaction to the alcohol.

"So, it's not something you have a prob…"

"…No." She assured me. "I used to think that I might've had an alcohol problem, but I'm quite sure I don't. Even when I asked my friends… 'What? Maya, you? You have nothing to worry about'. So, no. I don't have a problem with alcohol."

The issue was dropped.

The month before meeting Maya, my grandmother on my mother's side passed away. My grandmother and I had a psychic connection; she really understood me. While there was still a rift between her and my mom, with me there was no family stuff of any kind to cloud the relationship. It was clean: friend-to-friend, elder to initiate. It would have been JUST like her to orchestrate this cosmic meeting of my life partner. I always suspected her of having more influence and power than she knew herself. Feeling this sense of rightness, I buzzed the day I met Maya.

Even now, the buzz reverberates in my body as a distant memory. I can feel it right now.

After we married among the pine trees and under the arbor braided with sunflowers, we hugged the ministers goodbye. The best man and maid of honor laughed and smiled as they disappeared down the walkway from our house. With the smell of food and festivity still in the air, we just looked at one another. What now?

All the anticipation of getting married and the promises of being a good husband, a good wife—where did we start? How would we start?

So we played. We played like cats in the living room.

As a matter of fact, we played like cats on the day she died, too. It was snowing on that day in early November. We were almost three months into our marriage. The morning had been playful, loving, and fun. The afternoon was scary. I'd come back from lunch with a guy giving me tips on how to help my music business. I opened the, curiously, locked door. I called out to her as I walked into the kitchen. She emerged from her room looking distant, abstracted and maybe even a little drunk. Maya was fidgety, moody, and she had to leave. She had to leave right then and there.

"What's going on?" I asked.

"I've never seen you angry," she said.

"Yes. And. What's so bad about…"

"…It's not normal. It's…"

"...Maya, I haven't had anything to be angry about," I said a little too calmly.

"I can make you angry," she countered.

"Well, I'm sure you can. I doubt it, but I'm sure it's possible."

"I found your journals," she announced.

I paused and collected myself.

"I can tell you that I am a little surprised..." I managed.

"...and I've been reading them," she said.

"OK. I don't think it's right that you would do that. But I'm not mad. And really, I don't have a problem with it. But what I'd ask is that we read them together. You know, and talk about...

"...I've been reading them for a couple of weeks," she said, still trying to incite my anger. "And I've got them. I've got them all. And I'm going somewhere in my car and I'm not coming back until I've read every word so I can know exactly who my husband is. And you're not getting them back until I come back home."

"You, you took my journals and you're not giving them back?"

"That's right," she said.

Maya's eyes were glazed. She was altogether different. I was sure there was someone else in that body. And I wanted that person out of the house. The buzzing started again. The buzzing was an alarm.

"Wait, lemme get this straight—it's snowing, you're feeling emotional, and you've had too much to drink, you've hid my journals, and you want to get in your car and go driving?"

"That's right," she said, "and you're not stopping me."

"You leave, and you're not coming back," I seethed.

She had gotten the response she was looking for. She kept casting the net until she'd caught her fish. I could not believe the words came out of my mouth. They were foreign. They were ancient.

They were the words that would haunt me for years afterward.

"Don't go. C'mon now, don't go…don't go…don't…"

I clung to her ankle as she strode mightily toward the kitchen door dragging me behind her. She was an amazon. A super human. This was not the woman I had married. And I was not the man I thought I was.

Her car sped off down the dirt driveway as it snowed against the landscape made featureless by the low-hanging gray clouds.

CHAPTER 2

Wha…what?!

Written February, 2001

Maya had been away for a few hours when I was suddenly prompted to look out the back door. There, about a half mile away in the waning afternoon light, I thought I saw the flashing lights from a police car. The lights bleated through the branches of the scrub oak like a faint, rain-soaked heartbeat. I blinked and refocused my eyes, and they were gone. I watched as a few remaining snowflakes fell to the ground in the wake of the afternoon's snowstorm. Wiping a snowflake from my eyelashes, I shut the door behind me, still seeing the low-hanging gray clouds outside in my mind's eye as I continued through the living room and to my study.

The call came two hours later.

"This is Officer Lustig with the Oregon Highway Patrol.

Are you family to Maya Korenn?"

"Yes, I'm her husband."

Damn, she got a ticket for drunk driving, I thought. But wait, why the hell would he ask if I was family...don't they only ask that when....

"Could you come to the Rogue Valley Medical Hospital? She's been in an auto accident."

Maya lay on a gurney. Her impossible beauty lit the sterile ICU room. The respirator forced air into a chest that only hours ago had nestled close against me in bed. Hospital blood was replacing the blood she was losing internally. There was hardly a scratch on her.

"Sir, would you like to have her organs donated?" asked the young girl, impertinently snapping gum as she adjusted an IV tube. She kept an eye on the vital signs monitor with stunning nonchalance.

"Uh," I managed to say through my tears. My mouth agape and my mind spinning, I could only get an "uh" out. My face was wet. My body was crumbling. Minutes (maybe hours) before, two doctors had told me about her condition.

"She has a contused brain stem and massive damage to her internal organs," one of the doctors recited as if reading a report, "...and because of the damage to the brain stem, she will have lost all motor function...and even if we WERE to operate, she'd..."

"You mean she's going to....die?" I croaked.

They nodded solemnly.

I fell to the floor, grabbing at chair and table legs as I tumbled down into this abyss. Oh God, I'm falling. Lifetimes and faces were swirling around me in a maelstrom of voices and hums and tumbling blackness. I was sobbing with deep, wrenching animal noises that seemed to well up from a collective, far-away grief, a grief from all who ever felt the pain of loss.

Could I make a deal? Any kind of deal? My life for hers? No? How much? How much can I pay? Tell me it is a dream and I will do it right…I'll do it better… Do WHAT right? What did I do wrong *this* time? Where's the re-wind button? Let's re-do these last few hours. C'mon. Let's just do 'em. Somebody, get me to the fucking rewind button.

If I cry long enough, hard enough, can I trick the reality matrix? Trick it into rewriting the events of the last two hours and just give me my baby back? Give me my baby back. Just give my baby back. Please just make this so it did not happen. So it never really happened.

It didn't …did it? Did it?

The two doctors looked at me on the floor. There was a long pause as I looked up at them like a beggar, for I was indeed a beggar. And they were merely doctors practicing medicine.

"Sir?" pressed the ICU nurse.

"Uh, no. No thanks."

"Negative on the organs," she said dryly to an intercom in the room. She shot me an impossibly impertinent look.

It felt awkward and strange as I watched Maya's breast, visible through a buckle in the thermal blanket, as it rose and fell in time to the respirator's pumping action. Incredulous that I could even be thinking, "what a beautiful breast," I looked at her face and said, "baby…baby…baby…baby…….." My voice was drowning in the tears as they flowed down my throat, down my mouth, down my neck, down, down, down.

As Maya lay dying, she was the same as in life: beautiful on the outside, bleeding on the inside.

The ICU nurse told me that as long as her organs were not going to be donated, that we had best stop the flow of blood and the resuscitator. "Baby," I said silently, "they're turning off the oxygen …show them how you can breathe on your own….do it!"

I ordered her with every inch of my will to just breathe.

The oxygen was slowly reduced. This body double for Maya began struggling to get air. I say "body double" because the woman I loved was not in that body. Her lips began twitching frantically.

"Look," I yelled, "she's trying to breathe!"

"That's what dying looks like," the nurse said flatly.

"But….."

The heart monitor indicated a heart in spasm as the body fought fiercely before it gave one last gasp. And then… the muscles relaxed. The struggle was over.

The sudden silence was deafening. There was no sign of her spirit anywhere. I was sure it had flown hours ago, probably at the moment she'd collided with the cement abutment of the bridge less than a half mile from our house, less than eight hours before. She simply flew out of the car and observed as the glass and metal caved in on itself below her. Sparkly bits of glass showered the air in a constellation of stars. Pieces of paper suddenly sprang to life from the back seat. Hundreds of pieces of paper with dates and journal entries danced about the car. A flurry of objects floated and bounced all in slow motion. She regarded it all with a child's bemused curiosity and a yogi's detachment as the blond doll was tossed back and forth between the pillow-soft windshield, the pillow-soft seat, the rubbery, forgiving steering wheel, the gentle parking brake lever, the cushioned door window, and then peacefully, so peacefully, the rag doll relaxed as she sat slumped in the driver's seat.

Maya's lifeless form lay motionless. I looked at the nurse for an answer. "What do I do now?" Do I sign something? Is this where I fall to my knees and wail? Do I just walk out of here and leave her? This shell of my beloved? What about the papers?

What about her body?

It was minutes after midnight. My parents, who had stood by me for the last few hours, looked at me with the gravest concern. It was time to go home now.

"…..but….."

Time to go.

The hall lights outside the room were dimmed. Time to go. Time to go.

"…BUT!!!…"

I stayed with her long after my parents and our friends had left. There, in the dim light of the Intensive Care Unit with small, red LED lights casting ghostly shadows, I said goodbye to my bride. My wife. My friend.

The drive home was impossibly surreal. Life was going on as usual: impartial. Nothing had changed. The streets visible from the highway were lit with a seeming randomness. A lone truck driver barreled past me to keep to his schedule, his tail lights fading into the night as he sped ahead of me. At this sleepy hour, I was alone on the interstate. The tears had stopped and I felt relief. Relief that the ordeal was over. Relief that I had finally stopped crying. Things would be better now. They would… they would be better now.

"Good, I won't have to put up with her moods anymore," I thought. Moods?! Are you kidding? Those weren't moods, she had two personalities! Oh, and thank goodness I don't have to deal with her drinking anymore. God, remember when we were in that odd hotel above the square in Florence on our honeymoon and she guzzled that wine and became someone I'd never seen before? Who was that? A great burden has been lifted. It all happened for the best. I'm free. I'm free again.

"Hey Maya, I'm free again, I'm free. Maya? Maya, I'm… Where are you? Maya…? What would life have been like if you'd lived? A vegetable? A paralyzed vegetable. It's late and I'm thinking like a crazy man. Crazy? Talk about crazy. Now YOU were crazy, Maya. You were so extreme. You were so…and I loved that about you. Get over here. Be crazy again. I'm so tired. Be tired with me. I'm so very tired, Maya."

The gravel beneath my tires groaned and crunched as I pulled up to our driveway. The night was still. The house was expectant, as if waiting for an answer. I shut the garage door and plodded slowly along the long dark path between the garage and this behemoth of a house looming angular and unnatural in a rural and forested area outside Ashland, Oregon. The whoosh and clatter of the opening door danced maniacally off the walls and the rooms quivered. The house seemed to ask, "Well…where is she? What happened?"

"Uh, there was this policeman that called me on the phone and I went to the hospital and…."

It could wait until morning. The explaining to the house, our friends, her mother…. Everything would be different in the morning. I just needed to sleep.

I fell into bed, the enormous bed, now strangely unfamiliar and cold in an unthinkably large and lonely house. The lights on the hill out the bedroom window sparkled. Far in the distance, the two red lights perched atop the radio transmitter towers blinked out of sync. I watched them wearily, awaiting the few seconds when they'd pulse in unison. Two red lights beating as one red light.

I shut my eyes. Just before falling into a deep sleep, a huge heart began flapping its wings, hovering two or three feet above me. The beating of the wings was slow and sensual. Then this pulsating winged heart transformed itself into a nearly human-sized butterfly and observed me as it beat its wings with an imperturbable slowness above my head. I looked at it. It looked at me. I mouthed the name, "Maya?" A sweet tone emerged from the silence. And from the tone, a soft and unearthly light seemed to fill the bedroom. In that moment, everything was all right. The butterfly was there. My sweet butterfly hovering serenely over my bed. The butterfly lowered itself until it was nearly touching me. This supernal gentleness caused my body to drop into a luxurious deep sleep. No dreams to disturb or punctuate the sleep. Maya's butterfly presence watched over me the whole night. So profoundly deep. So soft. So relaxed. And so very far away.

It would be my last uninterrupted deep sleep for over two years.

Looking Back I
June, 2011

Jennifer: *Oh God, Michael, does rereading this feel real? Can you find the man who answered the phone to this news, saw his wife die, and found the strength to drive his car back home? The loneliness of it is breathtaking. I wish we could save one another from such pain. We don't get to, but I can't help wishing we could. . . . .*

Michael: *That man is buried somewhere. It feels like it was someone else's recounting of a life. But I also know that he's buried deep in my cells. And those cells are still wanting to scream out: "What on earth just happened?"*

It was the most surreal night of my life. The universe dealt me this unexpected card and I just had to deal with it. Just get on with life. That night, driving the 20 minutes back from the hospital, was like driving between two distant stars in the night in a foreign galaxy. And to watch the perfunctory and the mundane happening on that highway while my brain was in overwhelm added to the dream-like quality of it all.

It was like someone took the chess board of my life and with a deft and unstoppable sweep of a forearm, wiped the board clean with all the chess pieces falling in slow motion to the floor. And the floor was somewhere in outer space.

CHAPTER 3

Life less Maya

Written March, 2001

I woke up and sobbed as I walked down the stairway from my bedroom, hanging on to the wooden handrails for support. I wandered around the house, aimless and lost. The friend who had driven 11 hours to visit that morning left. I had told her I needed to be alone. Amazingly, she understood. The new paradigm was craziness. And people, well Donna in particular, seemed to understand. She saw me teetering on the edge of a precipice. She knew the look. Most everyone did. One does not question "the look."

I walked aimlessly around the house. Now larger than I ever thought, it waited for an explanation. I wandered from room to room to see if she was simply hiding out in one of the bathrooms. I opened my mouth and no words came out. Saliva and tears spanned the chasm of my mouth trying to utter a word…a sound. But, alas, no words. An animal sound managed to issue forth from somewhere deep inside my body. But that was it. There was no music in the house. The white walls looked gray. The once colorful pictures and art scattered on the walls were bled of their brilliant hues and had succumbed to this cold and colorless autumn day.

"What am I going to do today?" I thought. "I could brush my teeth. Oh, right…start a fire. It's cold in here. It's freezing in here."

And the day saw me routinely going about the absurd motions of starting a fire in the wood stove to keep warm. The biting cold outside rushed insensitively through the metal casings around the windows. There were entirely too many windows in this house.

My mouth was uttering inaudible names and phrases through the constant stream of tears. The house seemed helpless. Wordless. Music-less. Even the familiar creaks of the floorboards and joists seemed, somehow, silenced.

I drove to the big solid cement chunk of abutment on the road less than a mile away where her car had careened out of control. I hugged and kissed this big cement block of an assassin. For it was the last thing to touch her before she lost consciousness. Broken glass and bits of paper from her glove compartment lay as a stark reminder to what had happened in an instant the afternoon before.

That afternoon, people arrived. People I probably knew, but I couldn't see them. I saw their shoes. The shoes that shuffled past. The shoes that stayed right by me. There was a small confetti red heart on the tile floor that had, doubtless, fallen from a card that someone gave me. My eyes shifted from the shoes to the metallic little red heart on the floor. I watched shoes stepping on it, unaware that it was there. One shoe stepped mortally close to the innocent heart as I let out a gasp.

Maya's essence, for me, was in that heart. People were trampling this fragile heart. Unaware. Not tuned to her heart. And I couldn't speak to ask people not to step on the little red heart on the floor. The heart winked at me when it caught the light from an overhead light. No one noticed the heart. My eyes were focused on the heart and nothing else. The people were ghostly apparitions floating in and out of the house, but the red, metallic, confetti heart was all I could see.

"Honey, can I get you something to eat"?

Eat?! How could I eat? WHY would I want to eat? I was incredulous as to how a question concerning food could even come up. It was, quite simply, the very last thing on my mind.

I could drink though. "I'll have some water," I managed to whisper. I was thirsty. Unbelievably thirsty the whole of that afternoon. The tears. Their constant flow left me dry and caused me to think only about water. Water and Maya. Maya and Water.

Maya was a water person like I was. She was as much at home in the water as she was on an extended jog or camping in the mountains. We had planned to spend December in Hawaii. If there was a body of water, she was in it before I could even say, "Hey, d'ya wanna go in the…?"

My mother heated up a little bowl of soup for me, one that Maya had made for us. She'd made it to last us for several weeks. Most of it was frozen. She was still caring for me. Even from the other side.

I looked at the soup and decided that it was a crazed concept: eating. How could I eat when she was over there…just there, beyond the vaporous blue mist. "I can't live without you, Maya… don't get too comfortable going your own way, I'll be there. Hang on. I'll be right there. I just have to do this mourning thing first."

"Hello, Michael," people would say. I'd look up, though barely, to acknowledge them. But it was like looking at people from 20 feet under water. These watery apparitions waltzed in and out of view as I returned their "hello" with a sputter or faintly uttered "hi."

Like a camera aperture, a huge membrane opened near the bookcase where I was sitting in the kitchen. The unearthly, pulsing maw hovered patiently. I could go through this gaping hole if I chose. I had absolutely no doubt that I could walk through it and be on the other side. There was some doubt, however, whether I would be "allowed" to see Maya. Some astonishing presence of mind let me know that since I would be *choosing* to leave this body, I might not see her because she did NOT choose to end her life. That same presence of mind suggested that I might be placed in a different way station than Maya.

Then I looked at the confetti heart on the floor. It winked at me. The gaping rupture in this reality dream yawned and threatened to close. I knew that the time to walk through it was limited. The risk was great, but the payoff could be huge.

Certainly, the one priority at the moment was to keep from falling. My world was vertiginous, monosyllabic, and drenched in irrepressible tears. In this state, I was ready for anything but falseness. If I got any kind of pleasantry, such as:

"She's in a better place…" or "She's with the angels…"

I would go a little crazy on them. Nothing like a crazy griever. It throws people. They do not know what to DO with it. Besides, how the hell would THEY know where she was or with whom?

My rational side knew that these Hallmark niceties were spoken with the best of intentions, but my rational side was a memory. It was a reverberation in the distance. It belonged to another life.

I couldn't believe how awkward the whole affair was. It seemed that people wanted me to help THEM through it. They seemed to want me to help THEM know how to be with me, when all I really wanted to do was to throw up.

No sooner had the people come than they had gone. My parents were the last to leave. "If anything should happen to you, it would destroy me." It was all my mother could manage to say. Seeing her son in such a spectacularly desperate state, these were the only words my mother, helpless to help me now, could summon. And strangely, all I could now sense were people in their own dramas. And those dramas seemed petty and insignificant next to what had just happened in my life. I had lost my wife, and they were at a loss.

"Where is the little red heart…where'd it go…did somebody sweep it off the floor?" I thought to myself. I panicked. "I've got to be with her…and if not her, her picture." My eyes scanned the tile floor like a man possessed. The heart had disappeared. I collapsed in front of her picture and wept.

The Memorial Service

Someone had said, in a dream…or on the phone…or SOMEwhere, that they'd make the arrangements for a memorial service. "Why? Who died? Did Maya die?"

Someone walked me to a seat amid a sea of people. I saw my dad waving to me to come sit with the family…a vaguely familiar face bobbing like a man drifting in and out of view sinking into a trough… then lifted by a swell. "Ahoy" he seemed to be saying. "Ahoy there!"

This usher knows where I should be. I'll let this usher put me someplace. I couldn't sit with my family. I didn't want to sit with anyone. I wanted to be absent. I wanted to be in a softer place, someplace cloud-like and warm, where I could cry and be held. Instead I felt a flood of concern coming at me from all these people. People I couldn't look up to see.

I hung my head, looking down at the way my dusty blue wool pullover draped over my belt. I remembered how Maya had eagerly agreed with me about the soft simplicity of the pullover as I tried it on in the boutique in Italy 2 ½ months earlier. We had made a day-trip to Florence from our hotel in Assisi.

We had been married in Assisi, atop a rolling hill overlooking the smoky valley below. Warm summer days. Grapes swelling on the vines that draped over trellises everywhere. The delicious Italian salad of mozzarella, tomato, and basil with that wonderful olive oil…oh, and a little salt. The sweet smells of lavender and rosemary. Lavender and rosemary….lavender and….

And…

I sat down somewhere near the front of the Unitarian Church. Maya's mother was there. How did she get here? Oh, yeah. I rang her the day after I'd left the hospital. Did I really leave Maya at the hospital? Did I actually manage to find Maya's phone book and call her mother and father? Somehow, I still had the presence of mind to ring her family. Where on earth was I able to summon that kind of dutifulness within the middle of such a chaotic mental state? Oddly, I noticed how similar her wrists were to Maya's. She looked at me and seemed to hiss like a snake. Angry with me, with Oregon, with God.

Maya's mother, for reasons unknown, was asked to leave the Franciscan convent in which she was a Mother Superior. She met her husband soon after leaving the convent, and gave birth to Maya.

I was to find out after the memorial, that she was infuriated that I had chosen to have Maya's body cremated. (Did I decide that?...Was I given a choice?)

People spoke and people sang. There were even jokes. Many people laughed. I drifted in and out of actually being there. I was bereft on a restless sea. When I was present, I sat slumped, looking at the dusty blue pullover. It felt withered and lifeless, here in the cold of autumn. Like a fish losing its brilliantly painted opalescence when removed from the water.

I heard the local choir director sing "Let it be" at the piano.

Let WHAT be? That Maya's gone? I can't let it be. She's not gone yet. I KNOW that I can bring her back. She's just hiding out. Her soul slipped out of that body and it's right around here someplace. Maybe it's between the folds of the pullover. Here. Lemme look. No. But she IS here. SOME where. I know she is.

Suddenly I found myself hugging people as they lined up to greet me. I do not remember a single face. There were the smells of sweaters and jackets. Soft words. People crying as they held me. The intermingling of tears. Wet faces pressed against wet faces. Endless tears. It was a water world again.

Then I walked outside…alone or with many, I don't remember. The sky was bleak and gray before the service. Now, a full rainbow arched across a pale blue sky. It hung there, lighter than air, stretching the full length of the horizon. She's talking to me. The butterfly above my bed. And now the rainbow. At that moment, a buzzing shot up my spine. This tingling up the spine would be the only form of contact we would have again.

I would ask Maya a question. A positive or 'yes' answer came in an unequivocal energy burst up my spine. A negative or 'no' answer was a calm pooling of energy that remained at the base of the spine.

"Are you happy over there?"

Zing. Electricity shot unmistakably up my spine.

"Are you able to come back?"

…..

"Do you remember the time you ripped off all your clothes and jumped into the ocean ? Remember? We were camping."

…zing

"Are you near?"

Zing

"Do you know where you are?"

…..

"Do you still love m…"?

…zing, zing, zing

"How do I get where you are?"

…..

"Do you forgive me?"

Zing

"Oh God, I'm sad. Let me be with you. Can I be with you???"

…..

The day before the service, my parents took me to the wrecking yard to identify the remains of her car. We walked on gravel amid rows of automobiles ripped apart, mangled as if by an atomic blast. Then I recognized the nearly unidentifiable semblance of her sweet little red car. It looked as if a giant had stepped on it. "It's that one,"

I barely managed to utter as I fell to the ground. My parents did not know what to do with their disconsolate child. All my father was able to say was, "You need to see what happened."

His words drifted on the sea of my water world. This blurry water world. My mother dutifully removed Maya's personal effects from the car and put them in a bag.

And then, probably in the name of simply getting it all over with, we continued to the crematorium.

Who made these arrangements? Did I sign a paper agreeing to have her cremated? I couldn't remember anything. I was angry at the crematorium. I was angry at the people that owned the crematorium. And now, like Maya's mother, I blamed God.

I blamed God.

In the days following, cards came in. I only remember one of them. It said, "shit, shit, shit…I'm so sorry…"

The rest of them, I couldn't read. I tried. I could not read them. I don't remember what they said or who they were from. I do, however, vaguely remember airbrushed depictions of heaven… floral bouquets and ornate cursive lettering.

Now and again someone drifted through my door with food. Some incredible person, though I don't remember who it was, cleaned my house. But most of the time I was alone. Drifting around my cold house, I'd collapse on the floor and look at the images in the carpet or the swirling designs in the knotty pine wall of the sunroom.

The sunroom was her favorite room. It was bright, and it had been her idea to decorate it with the vibrant colors she loved. I could not seem to use color and get away with it, so I dressed the house conservatively. But she had taste beyond the mere "feminine touch." If I could describe her in one word, it would be "sunflower." Her face reminded me of a sunflower, a long-stemmed sunflower swaying gently back and forth in a soft breeze, caressing me, soothing me. Soothing me under the sun's warmth. Flowers and sun. Her sunflower presence and the warm sun that made her grow.

The phone didn't ring. It joined the rest of the mute fixtures in the house. I guessed that people were waiting for some kind of sign from me. All these people fussing over me…then, reality. I am alone. I'm completely a-frigging-lone.

It was a cold November. While I could ignore food and house-cleaning, I could not ignore that the house was growing cold. I'd hobble out to the woodpile and plod back to the house with a wheelbarrow of chopped wood. The red fox near the wood pile barked at me. The owl swung by my head with silent stealth and disappeared into the idly swaying pine trees on the other side of the house. Perfunctorily, I shuffled wood in the stove. I would watch the embers from a previous fire glow like angry little stars. I'd blow on them until I was in tears. What was the use? I was trying to warm a body that didn't really want to be here.

Looking Back II
June, 2011

Jennifer: *I can't imagine the searing public exposure of this memorial service, Michael. The awful fact of Maya's death was so new and raw, you were hardly here on the planet. You'd just been pulverized for God's sakes, how could anyone have thought it would be helpful to drag you through this? Did you ever feel angry at being expected to show up and answer for her death—to be the stand-in for everyone's horror fantasies of how it must feel to be widowed so new in love?*

I think I might have slammed courtesy into the "fuck you" zone—although, who knows? We're trying so frigging hard just to breathe, and maybe we're also inclined toward obedience because some part of us is still hoping to be good enough for our beloveds to choose to return to us--to life. That willing surrender to the collective courtesy, I can understand. Still, I am left wondering, how in the hell did you do it?

Michael: *I don't know that I did anything that day. I floated. Someone told me that there was a memorial service and I wasn't entirely sure who it was for. I don't think I did it out of courtesy to anyone, though I really see your point. I have lived much of my life motivated by a real or imagined need to be courteous. That day, however, courtesy was not in the picture. If someone had asked, "Are you doing this out of courtesy?" I would have answered, "Courtesy? Do I know this person, courtesy?" I was in an altered reality that dictated simply doing what I was told to do. I knew I was way the hell out there and that virtually anyone would have a firmer grip on the immediate social consensus than me. The denial and anger phases hadn't quite begun yet. I was still in shock.*

You know how when some part of you takes over when there is an emergency? You do things calmly, quickly and purposefully to get on the other side of the emergency. I know that I have urged a couple to get out of their car and successfully gotten them out seconds before their car was engulfed in rolling flames. Several times, I've stared into death's maw. For me. For others. Super-human mental acuity and physical power seem to take over in moments like these. The situation dictates an imperative. And, it's an imperative where there is no time to debate, consider or process.

Probably, that same section of my brain simply dictated:

"You're on overload. Let other people tell you what to do today. Even if you try, you will not figure out how to do anything social. Just let things happen."

Simply, I let things happen. My parents were furious with me for not sitting with them during the memorial service. Yet, I sat where the usher seated me. I'm sure people wondered why I made no eye contact with anyone. I could only do what I was told to do. Nothing more.

I know "shock" by heart. I see the hundred mile stare in veterans, widows, and accident victims. And shock, that day, was all there was. There was no room for anything else.

CHAPTER 4

Continue…Continue with What?
Written April, 2001

Everywhere I looked about me in the house, there was a reminder of her. A gum wrapper in the kitchen. A Kleenex. Her favorite chair. Our wedding picture in the living room. The plant she bought. Her rug. All these "things" with her energy IN them.

I had to get out of the house.

A few days later I got in my car, for which I'd just bought new tires, picked up the canister with her ashes in it, and drove. I drove north to find her.

I've italicized the following journal entries from the days following her death:

Saturday 12 November 1994
Portland, OR USA 18:15

Maya was taken from me on Wednesday, Nov 2nd. The ensuing days have felt dreamlike, the pain excruciating, the grief numbing.

I'm staying at the Gardner's house in Portland to just get out of Ashland.....to get away from the constant reminders. I've left a significant part of myself behind. I'm not much fun to be with: soft, introverted, selfish. I can't bear to be around joy and energy; it's simply too jarring.

The last 10 days have been unreal. The days and nights swim together in a dream reality. Am I dreaming? Did this all actually happen? I truly have a sense of life being a dream....and that real life is carried out probably on the plane where Maya is now.

Here I am at Randy's, half expecting Maya to call on the phone....so I can tell her I'll be home soon. The grief, like everyone said, comes in waves. I have moments of being my old self, and then it hits me. "I just lost my best friend...and she's not coming back..."

Monday 14 November 1994
Portland, OR USA 7:10

Dearest wife of mine, Maya-

Every moment of every day I replay our final moments together...how I'd have behaved differently.

If I could ONLY replay the right scenario in my mind, you'd come back. And I'd say, "oh sweetie, you would not believe the dream I had...but you're back, thank God you're back."

This was the most surprising aspect of the grieving, in retrospect. There was a certain logic and necessity to the process of replaying the events prior to her death. I was SO certain that if I could mentally replay the order of events in just the right way, she would slip back into this world. The accident, the hospital, the ICU nurse, the doctors…all of it never would have happened.

So replay I did. No fewer than thousands of times. If she'd looked left instead of right. If I'd gone down the stairs instead of up. If she'd tripped on her way to her car. If I'd insisted she not go. If I'd said, "I love you" like I always did when either of us went ANY where. If ONLY I'd insisted she not go. The guilt was an arrow in my abdomen slowly twisting. Like a game with an infinite number of possibilities, scenarios, and outcomes, I juggled the pieces like a scientist determined to have his eureka.

At the time, this was all very logical. It was my only hope. As I saw it, it was my only connection to a fast-disappearing friend. "Hang on Maya, don't go to the other side just yet…I've nearly got it figured out. I just wish you had shared all your fears and doubts with me, all of your dark side. And I would have shared mine with you. I did keep private, didn't I? Neither of us felt safe enough to share the shadows until the shadows chose you, my sweet princess and wife. They chose you."

Monday 14 November 1994
Portland, OR USA 17:45

I had trouble actually breathing today. It felt like something was sitting on my chest. I would make myself breathe and even as I did, I was swept up in a world of nausea. Today for the first time I felt like she left me. Left me here alone. Abandoned me. My friend. I felt I was cold out here in this strange world. Bereft with the old feeling of wanting to return to my harbor. My nurturer.

I wanted to race home. But the thought that she wouldn't be there was incomprehensible. I'm desperate for her. Wanting to make a deal with God. Just let me replay those few minutes. I'll give you my next year's earnings. I'll take years off my life. Make me an offer.

People have left messages on my phone machine to meet with me. I don't want to. I want only her.

I'm 45 years old today. I sound to myself like a 20-year-old. The same 20-year-old that spoke in such passionate and emotional terms so long ago. He's back.

Kathryn and Randy have been pampering me. Kathryn feeling Maya's presence constantly. Everyone is feeling her presence except for me. I want her here. Right here. I'm talking to Maya constantly. I wonder, even, if there will come the time when I speak to her not noticing the presence of others. Like a madman. And they'll look uncomfortably at one another and wonder where I went wrong.

Monday 14 November 1994
Portland, OR USA 22:20

Dearest wife of mine-

Missing you has become my full-time occupation. Preoccupation...and passion. But now, now 11 days after your sudden death, it almost feels like you never really existed. That you were an angel; an apparition that everyone saw and agreed upon. And I feel that somehow you knew it was coming. You clung tightly to me that night before. And in the morning, we made love in front of the pellet stove. You were saying goodbye and I wasn't hearing it.

'And I'll say good night to you my love.' My wife eternal.

Good night Maya.

Thursday, 17 November 1994
LaGrande, OR USA 6:25

Dearest sweet wife-

I finally really got the significance of your letter to me in Sedona. While there, I only quickly scanned it...never really appreciating the tremendous time you'd put into every thought, every word. I also recognized some hints of things to come with sentences like, "though I'm far away...and I really am, I'm really quite near..."

You were an angel sent to an unworthy student of your teachings and love. And I want every day to show you that I did learn. Every day to show you that I did and do love you; every day to show you that I'm going to work for you; write for you; compose for you and help heal the world for you. I'm going to finish what you set out to do. I'm going to heal people in the way you wanted to heal me.

I always complained how people just don't understand me. My complaint pales next to what was really true for you. People REALLY didn't get what you were about. They didn't see what you wanted for people. They were taken in by your beauty alone without ever seeing the angel there. The soft-spoken, wise and sweet angel there. And you know I'm not speaking metaphorically either. You know, and I know, that you are an angel. A real one.

No matter where I went, she was there sitting wordlessly in the passenger seat, even though her ashes were in a container in the back of the car on the floor. Like a genie, she'd loom out of the small confines of her sepulcher and, with child-like excitement, ask, "Where are we going next?"

I'd talk to her. "How are you doing? I'm sorry. I'm sorry you're gone. What's it like there? WHY ARE YOU NOT TALKING

BACK TO ME? Did you sign some kind of agreement? Do you only answer yes or no questions with spinal zings?

She seemed to sit wordlessly next to me in the car. Always excited to see something new. She was light. She was detached. She was non-thinking. She was like a child.

Sunday, 27 November 1994
Ashland, OR USA 22:35

Dearest wife of mine, Maya-

I woke up remembering how the night before you left, you clung tightly to me the entire night. Then you asked if we could make love in the morning in front of the fireplace. Then after breakfast you drew me into your mouth. You were so affectionate. You were trying to say goodbye. When you asked why I didn't have an orgasm in front of the pellet stove I said, "so I could keep yearning for you all day." I didn't know that it would be for the rest of my life.

I really didn't know how hard this would be. To be missing you with such an ache. To be crying constantly. Smelling your clothes and losing my mind. Regretting the way I didn't love you or understand you enough. But Maya, you can now be sure just how much I DO love you. I love you more than that which is imaginable...even to me.

I love you my dearest friend. I will write songs to you. I will write of my love for you in the sky.... I even am crying now. You knew all of this before you even left. I can tell by all the little messages that have been left behind for me to discover.

You knew a lot. A lot more than you were ready to share with me. I do hope you're well where you are. And you know I'd give anything to know just how you are doing. Please contact me, honey.

Monday 28 November, 1994
Ashland, OR USA 11:30

You did contact me. I heard you crying in the bed next to me in the middle of the night. Then I smelled the distinct fragrance of that oil that you had made for you. I know you came to me. You were probably right there in the bed with me, though I was too sleepy and dreamy to notice.

Thursday 1 December 1994
Ashland, OR USA 12:20

DREAM

Lying in a bed crying for Maya. A large black woman offers me a breast to suck on to pacify me. I think to myself that I know her husband and she conveys to me telepathically that it is OK anyway. But since what I needed was milk I begin to suck. In my mouth comes a Novocain-tasting liquid that numbs my mouth.

Women that I knew only peripherally would ask to come and sit with me. Women, not men. I must have been telegraphing an urgent call for 'mother.'

They would hold me as I cried. To my surprise, I'd be sexually activated. I would grasp and cling and they'd pull me to them. Even though it felt outlandishly inappropriate, it also felt like what I truly needed. This was comfort so visceral, and so inarguably an imperative of the moment, that it stood squarely in the face of whatever religious upbringing I may have had. And I dared anyone to point a finger at me. My body or this "soul's" need for female warmth was real, and true. And curiously, unlike any other time in my life, these female visitors held no other agenda in their touch but to comfort this embattled heart. It was a time like none other before or since and it was right out of Greek mythology.

Friday 2 December 1994
Ashland, OR USA 12:20

Dearest sweet wife Maya-

The missing you doesn't diminish. My respect, love, and reverence for you grows. The more I know, the more I love you. You are such a giving soul. And if, as one of the psychics said, you can read what I write to you over my shoulder, know now that I want the best for you wherever you are. That I infinitely appreciated your giving and loving nature. And that my love for you is eternal. I am crying now, as you can see. Tears of how difficult it was for you in this lifetime. Tears that I couldn't have taken the edge off of your pain...tears that I wasn't more advanced to actually be there more for you.

I have been picturing you lying there in the hospital. I say "you" though I know it wasn't you. But you had a glistening crystallized tear frozen near your eyelid. I kept waiting, watching for it to fall as I continually told you I love you. I kept saying the words, "I'm sorry... I love you," watching to see if the tear would fall. It just stayed there crystallized in your eyelashes. Were you crying when you crashed?

Looking Back III
June, 2011

Jennifer: *Oh Michael, as I read now, I see all our efforts to reconnect with them, to feel their ongoingness in our lives and at the same time, to bless their sacred passage to regions damnably unavailable to us.*

That mix was so compelling and so confusing—if we didn't know where they were, then we didn't know where we were. I guess we needed to wear ourselves out trying to find them, to offer gratitude for their having loved us, to ask forgiveness for the endless ways we fell short. Enduring the power of those feelings, Michael, was a full-time job. It took everything we had just to withstand the enormity of our own desperate desires and judgments.

Michael: *You're so right. We did everything we could to seduce the heavens into getting our beloveds back to us. And the guilt at not having been quite good enough as a partner! That was the killer.*

But there was one aspect in Maya's death I couldn't wrap my brain around. I knew and loved this person, and a singular mistake on a roadway claimed her body. But her consciousness couldn't have disappeared. Her essence couldn't be evaporated and nullified. Where the hell did it go? And where it went, I wanted to be there too or, at a minimum, have a sense of it.

As you know, Jennifer, marriage is a blending of the body, mind and soul triumvirate. I imagine that somewhere between mind and soul is consciousness. So why, why, why, when the body is taken, should the others dumbly follow? Is that a cosmological writ we are not privy to? It didn't make sense then, and it doesn't make sense now. But my mind's obsessive compulsion to know where Maya's consciousness went had me looking at just how feeble the tether to my own essence was. Were our consciousnesses still married, still going to have children, still planning a future together? Maybe that question, more than any other, had me probing the deeper questions emerging from the dizzying realization that her body was no longer one with her consciousness.

CHAPTER 5

Finding Comfort
Written May, 2001

I found sleeping more and more of a problem. I tried hot baths, valerian root, melatonin and acupuncture. Nothing could turn off the incessant machinations of a mind bent on striking some kind of deal with the powers that be to get this woman back here. Sleep, at best, was a fitful succession of half-waking-state dreams, monstrous and strange. I would get up and walk around the house, now hauntingly devoid of her vibrant spirit.

The only "things" that helped were bath salts, candles, food, and water.

My world became soft, perhaps like that of a migraine sufferer. Lights, quick movements, and sounds felt like bricks thrown through a plate glass window. Even the music that I once loved became a cacophony of reckless, dysfunctional, displaced emotion, except one.

To this day, I do not know what it was about the Native American flute that made it the only sound I could bear. It soothed me in a way that nothing else could. My ritual became a candle-lit bath followed by bed and music. I programmed the CD player in my bedroom to play the ethereal strains of R. Carlos Nakai as I was going to sleep. With a click of the remote, I'd be surrounded by the sound of a wooden Native American flute drifting around a reverberating landscape. I would imagine a lone soul perched on a rock in a large, deep canyon. I could feel the notes themselves, landing on every rock face, penetrating every crevice, warming every cell in my body. I'd be asleep before the end of the 50-minute recording. I wouldn't STAY asleep, but at least my mind would get a temporary reprieve from its incessant and obsessive meanderings.

It was a sound and an artist's interpretation that understood. It understood that some things just happen, that life in its drama will twist us and turn us if we allow it. Apparently, I did allow it. I saw no other option. I am now aware, however, that there is an option.

The sound was like a seamstress sewing the loosely woven fabric of my being into something whole again, however temporarily. It was the enchanter and the lover. It was God speaking to me through sound. By day's end, when this awareness that I called "me" was sprayed around my bedroom in a myriad disconnected fragments, I could click the remote and the shattered pieces of me would reorder themselves, gently placing my weary body on the bed. The energy of the flute's voice sang in my spine, soothing and understanding. Briefly visiting and comforting every chakra, the sound put each one of the faintly glowing chakra disks to bed. The sound penetrated my cells, sending a warming reassurance up my spine that home was still right here, in my heart. However difficult this was, it was not the end of all life. Like a mythological goddess, Nakai's music was knitting me back together again.

Music, always my mistress and enchantress, had now forged new meaning in my life. She had become my healer, my lifeline.

As a professional singer and composer, I use a synthesizer that sounds like a clarinet, oboe, or stringed instrument, and it has been quasi-convincing. But in the sound of this Native American flute, the breath of life was breathing itself through hollowed wood. It was breathing life into a grieving listener. I felt connected by breath itself—the miracle that connects us all to life in a body. With real wood eliciting a constellation of emotions for me, I became the listener. Before Nakai, I had always been the player, the performer.

Nakai's music was so very simple: a solitary voice wending its way through the uncharted territory of the soul, unaccompanied, singular and plaintive. It called out to the very nakedness of my soul. But there in the void was where the riches lay. It was where eternity spread a gossamer opalescence of limitless possibility before me—where my love was.

When I was not in a semi-trance state brokered by the sweet acoustic strains of one of the most ancient of musical instruments, life continued to be a painstaking ritual of mundane events.

Somewhere Warm

On bent knee before the woodstove, blowing embers with tears rolling down my bellowed cheeks, I wondered, "Why am I here? If I'm going to be a broken man, why not be some place warm, some place sunny?"

I booked a two-week trip in Maui. It was mid-December and couples and families strode everywhere along the beach. Every balmy night, I offered a ceremony to Maya at water's edge using candles and local flowers. Afterwards, I'd place the plumeria and jasmine in the lapping waves. I'd wave goodbye. I'd talk to Maya endlessly.

I didn't dare go to Kauai. That's where we'd planned to go backpacking the following month. Maui was overrun with tourists. I drifted into a Denny's: all this happiness, all this abandon, all these families, all this sound, all this color. I pushed some orange segments around my plate with a fork. I wanted to tell someone:

"You know, my wife died. And I'm feeling very miserable..."

At that point, I might have trailed off with unintelligible mutterings and been taken for a madman, but that's precisely what I was: a madman. I had lost my mind. With the exception of infinite repetitions of the death-day scenario, my mind was dead to me.

I had no desire for fruit or orange segments or color or fun or Maui or anything.

Drifting away from Denny's and hardly eating a thing, I swam a meditative breaststroke in the ocean, which was not as warm as I had hoped, but I could cry all I wanted. The salty tears became one with the great breast of Mother Ocean. "O Pacific Ocean Mother! Pacify me, soothe me, make me normal again. Tell her I love her." I could feel Maya's fingers all around me in the silken touch of the water against my skin. And she'd say, "There, there Michael." And I'd protest, "…but you don't understand. I'm dying here without you! How can you be so unattached, so nonchalant, so present, but not there?"

Noticing a flyer about a Christmas service at a Science of Mind Church, I went. I had never been to a Science of Mind Church. It was a breezy day on Maui's sunny side of the Island and a couple, walking in the parking lot toward the church with their long hair blowing in the wind, noticed and welcomed me. They sensed my being out of sorts. The aura of new love was all around them. Maya and I had it during the warm spring that we'd met. Then, too, the warm wind blew gently like fingers through our hair. It spoke of the promise of summer. The promise of discovering love anew.

After the service, they invited me to their home for Christmas morning. I made my way up to the house of the newly married, Patricia and Howard.

It was a few thousand feet above sea level and the warm Christmas air grew slightly cooler as I drove upcountry, carefully following their instructions to the modest and secluded home in this lush paradise. I left my rental car looking out on this expanse of the coast as I shyly knocked on their door. They were married only a week and already they had taken in a stranger to share Christmas with them.

The gesture humbled me.

After dinner they even gave me a present. I must have cried a lot that evening. I cried for everyone who had ever lost a loved one. I cried for the Joseph and Mary openness of this couple. I wondered if I would have done the same. Would I have taken in a stranger on Christmas morning a week into the marriage with my lovely new wife? No. I probably would have wanted her all to myself. Perhaps this was my punishment. Naw. Some things just happen. They just happen.

A few days later, the same couple, Patricia and Howard, invited me to a party. Many of their Science of Mind friends were there, many of them smoking grass. One woman implored me to let Maya go. Psychically, she'd received the message that Maya needed to be released. She thought I was holding on to Maya too selfishly. My recent gift of searing lucidity showed me that SHE needed to let something go. She had absolutely no right to be telling me how to conduct my grieving, particularly in her 'highness.' I was angry, angry with everyone and everything, so I did what had become very easy for me in this new emotional landscape called grief. I was uncomfortable, so I left.

I would let go of Maya in MY time and MY way and NO one would, could, or should advise me how to do my grieving. However long it took was going to be fine. For once in my life, I was going to lay claim to what was mine. MINE. This grief was all I had left of her. It was all I had, damn it.

"There has been enough crying. You need to let her go now. No more tears."

I was surprised by how many people said the same thing, even using those exact words. But I would let go when I was good and ready. Hanging on to this sadness was a way of hanging on to her: hanging on to her favorite dress, hanging on to her underwear that still had her magnificent scent. This was my only connection.

Everyone ELSE was telling me how they had been "visited" by Maya in their dreams. Everyone ELSE was telling me where she was and how she was doing. But me? I hadn't a clue. Maya seemed to be staying clear of me in my dreams, perhaps not wanting to give me too much hope, making an effort not to lure me too closely to the porthole.

Were there rules on the other side about contacting people on earth?

I remembered reading that Houdini said he would visit his wife once he was on the other side. They were avidly interested in the occult and the continuing contact of departed souls. But Mrs. Houdini, for all her faith and all her waiting, didn't hear from Harry. It was getting to be clear that I would not hear from Maya either.

Back at my vacation condo, the soft, dulcet caress of the ocean fell all around me, encasing me like welcoming arms. The scent of fragrant tropical flowers drifted and danced on the night air. I tumbled into bed and entered the strange, nocturnal world that, doubtless, every griever comes to know. The surreal quality of the day blended with an even more surreal dreamscape punctuated by sleeplessness, anger, and tears.

Tuesday 27 December 1994
Kihei Maui, HI USA 10:28

A roller coaster of a day. I discovered that I am constantly teetering between sanity and insanity. I'm hanging meaning and significance on everything that happens.

I went out on a snorkeling boat this afternoon. Everything seems a little boring. Like I've seen it and done it all many times before. Much of this trip was going through the motions, as if moving through this time period was the only important thing. Just get through Christmas. Get through the hard parts of the grief.

What do I have to look forward to when I get home? Skiing. Sorting through Maya's things and going to her storage locker...this is a dreaded thing for me. All the past pieces of Maya's life...the part of this wife of mine that I didn't even know. The wild thing that has actually occurred to me, yet I don't know how on earth I could really do it, would be to ask Maya's girlfriend, Mary, to pretend that she's Maya. Hold me. Tell me she loves me. I tell her I love her and make love to her. I realize that it sounds a little perverse. But there is a lot of perversity to this grief. Actually, much of it is perverse. Sleeping with her wedding dress. Talking to her as I masturbate. It's all so very wild. The concept is just so out of my ken. GRIEF.

A No Thing

The fabric of everything I knew had a loose thread. Traveling through time at the speed of light, the thread got caught on a cosmic metal shard of fate. And now, here in Maui, I was without the garment that defined my existence. I was a NO THING.

I became a raindrop when it rained. I was the sunshine when it shone. I was the sand beneath my feet. I was the soft, invisible presence of the air. I was nothing and all things, but an impossibly SAD no thing.

This may have been one of the most lucid times of my life. I experienced other people's dramas and personalities with searing clarity. The various social contrivances seemed hopelessly silly.

Though I had never tried it – wanted to but it scared the shit out of me – I imagined it was like being on LSD. Energy danced like the aurora borealis. Insincere people seemed like total buffoons. Fear seemed a constant companion of nearly everyone. Sound had color and movement scripted within it. Animals and children were the only ones that made any sense to me.

Almost immediately following Maya's death, a cat showed up out of nowhere and just hung close to my house for the first few weeks and then disappeared, never to be seen again.

When I first moved into my Southern Oregon house, the deer would often listen to my piano-playing. They gathered near the front door and looked in as I played. The vibration seemed to interest them. Otherwise, the deer meandered a respectful distance away from the house. But for weeks after Maya's passing, a single doe stayed close around the house even when I was not playing the piano, sensing my need. No sudden sound or movement caused her to shy away from this seeming vigil; she stayed right by the house a few feet from me, regarding me thoughtfully.

A year or so later, I noticed that a fawn had suddenly disappeared. They never left their mothers' sides. The doe stared at me the morning her fawn vanished. We locked eyes. She couldn't have been more than 10 feet away. Though we stood there many species and understandings apart, I knew what had happened and I knew she was asking, "Oh God, this pain...what do I do?" If a deer can look bewildered and sad, this one most surely did. A crystallized tear hung on her eye.

Me and Women

"O, swear not by the moon, the fickle moon, the inconstant moon, that monthly changes in her circle orb..."
-William Shakespeare

What IS it with me and women?! Women have always been my crucible.

Each and every time I have ever been abandoned by a woman my life has been thrown into an emotional maelstrom. And this was the grandest of them all. This was the abandonment of all abandonments. An actual death. At once incomprehensible and painful beyond description.

The great mercurial and mystical Moon Goddess has always been my teacher. The mystery of the feminine. The changeable woman. The Mona Lisa. The quixotic nature of the feminine.

CHAPTER 6

Ashes

Written May, 2001

Back home from Hawaii, I was faced with the reality of actually making sense of all her belongings and her financial affairs. I did NOT want to do it, any of it.

I sleuthed through her address book, feeling like a thief. I had always practiced such respect for others' private things. Nonetheless, I perused her journals. I was looking for clues as to who she was and who her closest friends were. I felt that her closest friends would want to be included in this ceremonial releasing of Maya's possessions. So I rang them all and asked if they wanted to sort through her clothes and belongings with me.

Weeks later, two of her oldest girlfriends appeared at my house. We went through all Maya's clothes, jewelry, and furniture. I cried when an object triggered a memory. As I supervised the ransacking of all her worldly possessions, I was coming to know the woman I married. We had been too busy enjoying ourselves and examining what it was to be in a relationship to really get to know each other. But now, little by little, in the voyeuristic role of reading her journals and address book, I was piecing a life together. It was the only way I could hold on to her.

Maya's two girlfriends and I boxed the bulk of her clothes with the intention of donating them to a local shelter for battered women. I read every little scrap of paper in her coat pockets. The notes to herself, the spare change, the single earring, the knick-knacks everywhere…they all felt like a piece of this woman. I gave pieces of her jewelry to each of Maya's friends for their help. We spread some of her ashes underneath a natural arbor made by the pines in the back yard—the very spot where Maya and I were married. We sang "Amazing Grace." (What is it about that song, anyway?) We each, in turn, spoke to her. We spoke of all the things Maya was to us. We expressed our love and gratitude at having had her in our lives. Then we released her.

I was so grateful to her girlfriends for having pieced together a fuller picture of who Maya was. I felt lucky to have them. And they felt grateful at having been included in this sacred "goodbye."

Monday 16 January 1995
Jedediah Smith State Park, CA USA 3:07

Watching the Smith River run swollen with weeks of rain run-off. Feeling Maya in the tall redwoods overhead. Reflecting on two days of trying to put together Maya's leaving.

I don't know what it is about being in a vulnerable emotional state but people just appear in my life. Last night, this woman that was a friend of a friend said to me that Maya needed to leave in order for me to do all these things that I needed to complete, that we had made a pact to do it this way. She said that pain is the ONLY way we learn, the only thing that shakes us up enough to let the learning in. What I had to learn was so important that the death of my soul mate was the only thing that would assure my learning.

This all makes sense. But it's simply immaterial. It's useless information in the final analysis. We're here now. While the big 'new age' picture may offer temporary balm for the lost and restless soul, the hurt and the emotions still need to be dealt with.

I seem to no longer fear death...or even fear itself.

Maya lives within me now. She was always the one that went on long walks with me when I thought I was alone but suspected that perhaps I wasn't.

I got a card from a lady I don't know who channels Mother Mary:

"Michael, this is Mary. Your Mother. Maya is with me now. Maya was a gift to humanity. She was one of my bodies. You were twin souls. Maya was a soul that couldn't understand the sorrows of illusion. Twin souls usually work with one on the earth side and one on the other side. Maya needed to be on the other side. You are one flame."

Friday 17 February 1995
San Francisco, CA USA 4:23

The strange dichotomy is that my heart is as open as I am angry. I am as loving as I am hateful. I am as understanding as I am not.

It's a time of extreme emotions.

This is the beginning of an unimaginably new and different phase of my life.

I so clearly feel a falling away of the old personality.

The heart connection that Maya always spoke about as having been key to who she was is now who I am. My only interest is in being real. Heartfelt. No shackles on my heart. No protection. I want loving to be as natural a part of me as breathing.

I went to the ocean to spread her ashes. Again, I imagined her seated right next to me in the car, eager to see the ocean as it revealed itself through a cleave in the mountains. She looked at me like an excited child, with her mouth forming an incredulous "Oh."

Wide-eyed, childlike, and detached, she watched as I carefully found a sheltered spot on the beach where I could light candles and reverently place them on either side of her picture.

This was the same beach where we had camped a year before. I'll never forget my incredulity as she stripped off her clothes and went running into the surf. The spring sun hadn't heated the air enough to make the thought of swimming inviting. Just the thought, alone, of jumping in the water made me give a hypothermic gasp. On the other hand, Maya became a gazelle, staccatoing across the shallow surf and plunging into a forceful, ragged wave. Her fearlessness took my breath away. As un-inclined as I was to be one-upped by anyone having anything to do with the ocean, I held back and watched with slack jaw. She cavorted like a seal, running back out of the surf with every light in her body switched on. She was laughing as bits of seaweed clung to her ankles and hair. She was a mermaid! She was Aphrodite emerging from the sea for her morning bath. She was a lunatic. She was the woman that slept with me in the tent.

I fell in love with this woman in that very moment.

Now that same shore looked desolate and lackluster. I struggled to keep the candles lit in the gusts of wind. I spoke to her picture as she just stared back at me. I told her how angry I was, how very much I missed her, how abandoned and hurt and shocked and lost I was. She stared back, forever patient, forever listening. "Get it all out, Michael," she seemed to be saying.

I took her ashes to the exact spot where she had played in the freezing cold waves. I threw them into the surf. The last of her ashes fell like a ghostly waterfall. A wind snapped them up into the air and blew some of the ash into my face. My beloved's ashes flew into my opened mouth, and rather than spit, cough and sputter, I let them stay. I let them stay so I would forever remember.

CHAPTER 7

The Healing
Written June, 2001

With the exception of "A Grief Observed" by C.S. Lewis, much of what I read about grief did little to assuage the trauma and sadness of my beleaguered self. Most of the books I scanned dealt with grief in a thinly disguised clinical voice. They were removed from grief's madnesses and vicissitudes.

Friends were at a loss for how to be with me. Couples seemed to avoid me because I reminded them of the grim possibility that existed for them. Loss was like a virulent contagion that couples, in particular, could catch. No one wanted any part of the disease that had left me a desolate and spouseless leper.

What finally offered real help were two grief support groups. I figured other grievers would understand my surreal spin on reality, but it was a stretch for me to reach out to a 'group' anything. I'd always found the homogeneity that seemed to characterize any group stultifying. No singular voice would be able to emerge from the agreement to simply BE in a group.

Nonetheless, I was desperate to talk to others who had sustained the loss and exhibited the look. I was quite sure that the only people who could truly understand the gravity of this experience were those who had made the same or a similar journey.

I found a group that attracted grievers of all shapes and sizes: a young lady who had lost her horse, a man who had lost his mother several years prior, a lady who had lost her daughter. The enormously divergent types of losses notwithstanding, they all had *the look*—the glazed look of a soldier after combat, the immigrant coming to the United States during the potato famine, the prisoner of war, the jilted lover. These people understood. Even the facilitator had the look. Repeated losses had etched their mark deeply in her brow and tugged relentlessly at the skin under her eyes.

We wore nametags. We talked about the person we'd lost. As one person began to cry, it inevitably set off a chain reaction. There was no room for pretense or guise here; this was where the ravaged heart was put in the middle of the circle and everyone cried about it. The heart stripped of its armor. The personality stripped of its pride. The raw person – naked and shivering.

What I felt in the group was the expression of unexpressed universal grief. It didn't matter if one was articulate or speechless. The look and the tears were the same, and they spoke volumes.

Week after week, we made our ways to this sanctuary and sat in a circle that became grief's womb. Here it was OK for men to cry. Here it was OK for us to stammer, to choke, or to even float off. We lit a candle to our beloved and sang:

> *Friend, I will remember you*
> *Think of you; pray for you.*
> *And when another day is through*
> *I will remember you.*

Although it felt hauntingly like kindergarten and at times I felt vulnerable and silly, there was something vaguely healing for me to simply admit to this huge pain in front of others. Like the recent spate of talk shows where people admit to their most extravagant and closeted secrets before millions of viewers, somehow exorcising their demons and feeling absolved, the bewildered person bereft on the sea of loss seems similarly pacified by a peer group as witness.

Just like those who had no idea how to comfort me at my time of loss, I had no idea how to reasonably face the multi-layered, complex aspects of my own grief. It wasn't just my grief at having lost this friend-lover-wife; it was all loss through all time. Maya had awakened me to—drawn my attention to—my loss of innocence. And the myriad losses since childhood. She had switched on my awareness to all the little losses that blend into the big fat cumulative loss.

Who the hell was this mystery teacher, Maya—this person who blew into my life?

> *Maya is the principal deity that manifests, perpetuates and governs the Universe.*
>
> —Wikipedia

This is the person I met, married, and lost all within the same year. She was a fire that burned through every part of my life; nothing was left without its marking singe. And in the burning, the ashes were left as an offering to my soul. Was she an illusion? Was she a dream of duality in the phenomenal universe?

I continued going to grief group meetings in a stark commercial building in a nearby characterless town. Then someone mentioned to me that an informal group of grievers assembled weekly and locally at someone's house. Would I want to check it out? I checked it out. All widows. This was more in line with what I was looking for originally. They had all lost spouses. Although I kept going to the other meetings, I began attending this group as well. That's when I learned the word, "widower." Now I knew what I was. I was married barely three months and I BECAME a widower!

The six women in the group had lost their husbands several years previously to long-term illness, tragic accident, sudden illness. I brought the raw immediacy of loss back for them; they returned to the throes of their deepest sense of loss as if it had happened the day before. Although the look was not so apparent on their faces anymore, the memories tugged at the brow, eyes, and mouth while they temporarily revisited the pain. The pain for most of them, though, had receded considerably over time.

Time. Ah yes. The magic healer. I wanted the magic healer of time to put me to sleep for six years and then awaken me suddenly. But not feeling was not where I was. My face would contort as I recounted the agony of the loss through the tears. My voice would dip into registers unknown to me. The trapped animal inside my chest would heave and groan as the women listened patiently. They seemed to have endless patience and understanding. They were not in a hurry for me to heal. *They knew.* They knew ALL about the slippery terrain of loss, for they had all slipped and fallen and picked themselves back up again several times.

I explored my abandonment. I explored the anger of feeling abandoned. I explored the sleepless nights. I explored the increased libido. I explored the sadness in simply missing her. I explored the gaping hole in my heart. And they understood. These women, with whom I ordinarily wouldn't have a lot in common, understood exactly what I meant. The incomprehensible magnitude of the shared trauma opened the dialogue for all of us. I credit much of my healing in this period to both these groups. There were times I just wanted to leap up from my chair and kiss them all. Kiss them for their bravery, courage, rawness, softness, and humility.

Jennifer

Four months after Maya's leaving, I summoned a kind of mock enthusiasm to put together a musical I'd written. I queried the local choir director (the one who sang "Let it Be" at Maya's memorial service).

"Dave, do you know any good, 12-year-old boy singers for my musical?"

"I do know one boy," he said, "…he's good, very good, and this might even be a good time for him to be involved in something. He's younger than what you're looking for. But, um…he just lost his dad and he's having a hard time. So, like I said, this could be a good time for him to do something like this."

I walked down the aisle of the Methodist Church where Galen was with his mother. They were huddled around an ebony grand piano. I introduced myself to Galen and Jennifer. Galen looked like an English schoolboy. Porcelain and rosy-cheeked, he had the abstracted look. He avoided eye contact and hovered closely to his mom, seemingly frail and tentative.

"…Michael, and you are…Jennifer?"

Her elegant frame stood beaten and unsure as we shook hands and took each other in. Her forehead was a topographical map that said, "How could this have happened to us?!" She seemed to be looking for energy from the piano…from the air she was breathing…anywhere she could get it.

"And his dad was your husband?"

"Yes."

"When?" I asked.

"Beginning of December," she replied, staring over my shoulder as if Gordon might suddenly appear there.

"I lost my wife the 2nd of November."

We stared at one another as the tears welled. Reading each other, we recognized the familiar ache.

"You know, I'd…I'd just like to hear Galen sing a couple of intervals from the piano…" I said, breaking what would most surely have become a chain reaction of tears.

"We have a song he could sing for you," she interjected.

"Well, that would be great…you can accompany him?"

She nodded.

Jennifer sat at the piano like it was an old friend. And this friend seemed to hold her together. She sat with an elegance and command of the instrument. And the piano knew, like a horse knows about its rider, that she was now in control. The piano was an extension of the unarticulated part of herself. The part that had no words, and if it did, would need be in Sanskrit or Aramaic.

Jennifer gave Galen a nod that it was "OK" to sing now. Galen's voice had the bell-like ring of a Viennese choirboy. He sang with impeccable pitch and a stunningly accurate British accent. It was a song from The Secret Garden. He became that innocent English boy to escape the impossibly difficult task of being a Southern Oregon boy who'd just lost his father. His ethereal strains flew high above his own earthbound grief. Watching the boy beneath him on an island of loss and despair, the ruddy-cheeked boy overhead circled as he soared and dipped through the clouds. The tones, like the pure sound coming from a fine crystal goblet struck by a felt hammer, hung in every rosewood corner of the church. Winging his way in the company of cherubs and angels, a fanfare of trumpets announced the coming of this joyous choirboy. With a final dive, the winged boy became one with Galen standing close to his mother at the piano. Galen looked up, though not at me, when he finished singing. The flight was over. He was back in the body. He was back in the impossible thick of it.

"I think he'd do great…is he available for rehearsal early next…"

As I was speaking, I was seeing this woman collapsing before my eyes. Galen stood by her as if to prop her up. They were both being strong for each other, Galen more on autopilot than his mom. They seemed like a J.D. Salinger mother and son team, bound together by blood, common experience, and an uncommon sensitivity borne of keen intelligence.

This was what we both needed. Not a group, though I continued going to the groups, and not a book about grieving. We needed one-on-one contact with each other. Both of us being musicians made for a gigantic leap forward into our common experience. With this, we began meeting over dinner or lunch on a somewhat weekly basis. We'd give voice to the otherwise silent world of grief. As our partners seemed to sit thoughtfully listening, we gave the grief we'd come to know better than any body part, an anatomy. Gordon and Maya sat patiently observing with, what I could only guess to be, academic curiosity.

Our meetings covered the specifics of what happened immediately before the moment of death, how our lives were thrown up into the air, and how the pieces landed with randomness and seeming indifference. We both had an overriding sense that justice was absent in our moments of loss. And this is where we got caught and derailed, because where divine justice has absolutely no stake in earthly justice, this mind still wants an explanation; it demands one. With fists shaking at God, we wondered if He truly existed. And if so:

Why? Why? WHY?

How could He stand by and let something like this happen? What kind of God can You possibly be to allow this? War! Natural disaster. And now my life has fallen apart. Damn it all anyway!!! I can't even meditate anymore. When I close my eyes, she's right there beside me, meditating with that angelic focus on her face. The smell of her hair. Her intense focus.

I try to reach You. I try to FORGIVE You and I can't. I just can't. My life seems an accident. My wife left me, and You've deserted me. Etc.

In our discussions we tried to separate out the ease with which we could slip into a victim's perspective, and the grander view of simply acknowledging that shit happens. That all of this probably had nothing to do with God and everything to do with what we, as souls, signed on for. What we, as souls, wanted to facilitate in embracing greater love and expansion.

It all sounds so…so *current* now. The current thought has answers for everything. Everything is perfect just as it is. There is a divine perfection in everything that happens. Yeah, well, meanwhile, it hurts. And none of these words about divine perfection help one wit.

A richness emerged from the ashes of these two disparate lives navigating out of tragedy. A friendship, whose genesis was salty tears and running noses, became grist for something a little more real and a little deeper than the temporary and, somehow, superficial connection of stage mother and music director. We alternately pulled one another out of grief's quicksand. We coaxed each other away from four-story open windows. We laughed at the sanity that lives, somehow, within insanity itself. We struck out at the illusion of life and death. We laughed at the silliness inherent in a person's drama, or worse yet, the intermingling of dramas as they greet each other on the stage of the absurd. We talked about the wild and woolly ways that we, as society's junkies, hug close to the cultural trance and get our drugs from the local fixer: television, the newspaper, magazines, anxiety and depression meds, movies, the news and whatever else seduces us away from seeing who we are and where we are going.

Jennifer and I gave form to the formless world of bereavement. In doing so, a friendship was forged out of tears and wrenching guts that crashing worlds could not shake.

Dancing?!

I had begun to bore myself. I was probably a rather frightful prospect for others to spend time with as well. I floated in and out of being sullen and moody. This grieving business had few apparent silver linings. Of the few silver linings, my weekly talks with Jennifer and the ever-faithful sound of Carlos R. Nakai's flute became islands of sanity in a world completely insensitive to this very particular sadness.

In grief's joyless landscape, there was no excitement and no radiance. Therefore, I contrived to find something that would restore my former spark, if for only a few moments. After all, like my brother and sister, I was voted class clown by my high school graduating class. Where was the clown, the buffoon, the prankster?! Certainly he was hiding under a rock somewhere, waiting for the heaviness to clear.

Dancing seemed to be one of the most obvious ways to entice radiance back into my eyes. If I could not resurrect my slumbering joy while dancing…well, it wasn't going to happen at all. I signed up for an east coast swing dance class. While memorizing strings of steps was challenging, I soon caught on. A smile would sneak across my face when I made a mistake, and a full-fledged beam would overtake my face when I would actually dance to a whole song.

Little by little, the music found its way to my feet and body. The music of the Big Bands shot its time-honored adrenaline and vitality into every one of my body's cells. Count Basie and Duke Ellington worked their rejuvenating music magic on this tired body of mine. My very atoms readily responded to the entreaty and, finally, the imperative to shake it loose. Once the basic moves were down, my body began rejoicing in its own aliveness again. For the first time since that fateful, cold and gray November evening, I began to see how free and airborne my spirit could be. Finally, I realized—I had a whole life ahead of me. It became possible that I could have a life in which I could play and dance and celebrate and make love and swim and laugh and sing.

Not altogether unlike dancing, when I was 10, I'd go to the local park and swing on the rings and do front and back-flipping dismounts called fly-aways or front-to-backs or jerk-backs. The fleeting moments in the air while the body rotated before landing were not only profoundly in the body, but sweetly in the moment. I liked the way my body felt as it reveled in temporary weightlessness above the sand pit. I liked the idea of flying away. I liked the ecstatic moment when my hands released the metal rings and the air whistled through my fingers.

Swing dancing became the high point of every week, as I flew away on the dance floor. If I needed a drug to disentangle myself from the clutches of sadness and self-obsession, I let dancing be my drug. It was impossible not to smile when swing dancing. The marvel of the feet doing all manner of footwork in total disassociation from or respect for the brain was a coup of immense proportion. I was saying, "I want this joy in my life. I'm entirely too exhausted dealing with the facts. The facts happened, but they're not happening now. O nefarious mind, take a vacation away from me. My attitude is all I have to fashion my perspective. Mind and its weighty baggage—be gone!"

And gone it was, on Tuesday, Wednesday, and Thursday nights.

Dancing did a world of good to heal my sadness.

Alternative Healing

When I could barely breathe for the weight on my chest and dancing was days away, I would go to see various healers. I placed my life in their hands—energy workers, acupuncturists, naturopaths, shamans. No alternative healing stone was left unturned.

I lay on my back while my acupuncturist cleared energy blocks with, seemingly larger than necessary, needles and warming moxibustion. I looked at the same mosaic of pictures on his ceiling during three dozen sessions. Could I discover yet another picture or design, one that I had not seen before? A picture of a mountain goat was perched high on a ledge looking warily at the photographer. What part of the picture was I?

Another picture was of a deep forest in winter. What happened to me when I put myself in this forest? I thought of the unconscious. I thought of death. I thought of loneliness. There were pictures of a Middle Eastern girl, a child, an old lady, a lake, a stream, a meadow. I was so open to suggestion as I let the emotions bubble up from deep within.

"Ow," I'd say, as one of the needles intruded on my reverie with its distinctive sting.

"You may feel spacey after this, be careful."

And sure enough, I was. I had absolutely no idea how it worked, but it did. I was told that the body had several energy highways called meridians. Traffic jams in the energy flow caused imbalance, emotionally and physically. Just how many treatments would I need until I would feel normal again?

The more I went and the more different types of healers I went to, the more it became clear to me that the body-healing circuit could be its own addiction. Sooner or later, I was going to have to take matters into my own hands.

And I did.

CHAPTER 8

Growth
Written July, 2001

I had decided to fashion a healing forged by my own intuition's authority and the guess that no one knows better than I do what this mind-body needs.

Perhaps I could take charge of this healing journey by composing music that would heal me. I could deal with my grief, my sadness, my rage, and my feelings of utter loss and abandonment through music. It would spring from my deepest inner knowing about what, exactly, I needed to do to cycle more effectively through these feelings. Music would help sanctify this passage. I had never lost anyone, and I needed a road map. I was not finding the sought-after roadmap in books, in grief research material or anywhere else. I would create my own.

It started out as a musical commemoration of Maya's life and my love for her. I composed songs that reflected all the ups and downs of having lost her. In most cases, I wrote the songs uncharacteristically away from the piano. Quite a few of the songs came to me during early morning walks along a certain stretch of beach in Hawaii and others on long road trips. My hand recorder was always at my side ready to record my every melody or lyric idea.

But it grew into something far more compelling. It became the controlled environment in which I needed to flail and scream and weep and ponder.

I spent the better part of a year compiling the songs. Each one represented a different facet of my grief and my love for Maya. The music swam in the murky and unknown depths of my sadness. No language could utter the feelings that seemed so effortlessly conveyed in music's sanctum. The cellos would pulse with the soul's imperative to weather all adversity in love's name. The pizzicato strings gently underlined and provided punctuation to music's most tender words. The round warm sounds of the oboe, clarinet, and bassoon entered my body with the same inexorability of the Native American flute that soothed me to sleep each night the first year. The penetrating tones bored into my veins and bones—ever calming, ever soothing, ever loving.

The melodies swirled about me every moment of every day, the resonance of the deep bass rumbling my belly and the ethereal upper tones softly vibrating my face and throat. I spent hours at the keyboard, massaging my body and mind with the sound and vibration of undulating chords lolling me back and forth, rocking me in the unique cradle of music's complete understanding. It was my obsession; I was healing myself with this music. No one could have done it better. Although I have sworn that Chopin has literally entered my dreams with his sweet chromatic descents down the piano (and what softer caress than his Piano Concerto in E Minor, Opus 11), my music was so profoundly personal that my cells stood alert and applauded.

I recorded all the instrumentals over the course of a year. When it finally came time to add the voice, I stood before the microphone and was shocked to discover that I was barely able to sing. My voice had no range and the vocal cords slipped in and out of their former reliability. I sounded like a teenage boy at the awkward stage of his voice change.

I saw a throat specialist and he told me that I had developed a growth on my vocal cords. Not nodes, but a growth that needed to be excised.

"Do you smoke, Michael?" asked my doctor.

"No."

"Michael, you can tell me…do you smoke…anything?"

"No," I insisted.

"This growth would certainly suggest that you smoke," he insisted.

"Well, I don't smoke. What do I have to gain by lying?" I asked. "I just want to get rid of this thing."

"This thing" was the reason I couldn't sing. Once removed, I would probably be able to sing again.

Over the next six months, I tried all forms of alternative therapies. I faithfully followed an Ayurvedic regimen and every conceivable natural protocol I could find. Nothing worked. I still could not sing, and my speaking voice had become embarrassing, even painful at times. My voice would crack and I had no control over it.

As if in a horror movie, an acupuncturist placing a needle near the growth on my throat was thrust across the room when my throat involuntarily gave a violent twitch.

"Whoa, now THAT'S never happened before," he said as he gathered himself together. That is when I understood: this was grief stuck in my throat. I still had heaps of expressing to do, and the grief was going to stay there until I dealt with it. The energy was literally caught in my throat. No acupuncturist or naturopath was going to get rid of it. It would go in its own time, when IT was ready. Quite literally, I had a lump in my throat.

After nearly a year of alternative efforts, the throat doctor suggested I was a fool for not simply getting it cut out. As a last ditch effort to get my voice back, I submitted to the surgery.

A few of my friends came to see me off as I roamed the halls in my silly hospital gown with my butt hanging out the back. Damn, I hated surgery. The anesthetic. So strange and spooky.

After surgery, I awoke gasping for breath. That swimmy netherworld of recovery had me looking at the porthole again. "I could walk through right now," I thought. "Nah," I concluded, then drifted off again.

I didn't utter a whisper for the following week. I spat blood for the first few days. I visualized my throat's health, surrounding it with light. I even placed a picture of my throat on a prayer altar. I praised it for all the good work it had done. I would make sure my voice came back.

Incredibly, the post-operative check-up two weeks later showed that the same growth was there. The doctor moved away from his scope in disbelief. Same size. Same place. Same thing. He swore that he had removed it. It was a horror movie.

How could it have come back? It surely had nothing to do with vocal misuse, for I had barely uttered a word since the surgery. But it was there once more. Now I had to live with the possibility that I might never sing or talk again because of the growth that would not go away. My voice became croaky and continued to get worse.

Who was I if not a singer? Who was I if not a speaker? Was there anything left? Life without a voice was unthinkable.

It was at this time that I gave real consideration to my self-image. The picture I had of myself was that of a singer/composer and, oft times, speaker. What would life be like without my signature?

Life continued within the soft confines of judiciously spoken words and no singing. Who am I with no voice? Am I my hands? My writings? Am I a lover? A dancer? A clown? A friend? A loaf of bread? Who AM I?

The stillness of the abyss swept over me. Nothingness. Damn it, Maya, look at all this stuff that is happening to me. Why did you have to leave? We could have had a child by now. You could be painting and doing your therapy practice and I could be writing lovely songs about you…and nature…and the ocean…and we'd be loving this magnificent child together…..

A year had passed since the surgery and I went to another throat specialist as my voice began to improve somewhat. She said the growth was gone. No growth?! But who am I without…. Shut… UP! There is no growth!

I was happier than I had been in years. No growth. I went to the grower's market in town and hugged everyone I saw. I was a man absolved. A man possessed.

Immediately, I threw myself back into recording the vocals for Maya's CD. I eased into it at first and then sang full voice. It was back.

One song simply repeated "I miss you." While the chords shifted restlessly under the one plaintive cry, the song became a sort of primal scream. I placed myself in front of the microphone as the tracks played and let myself sing, "I miss you." Originally intended as an instrumental, the melody very simply voiced the three syllables of those three words. But as I began singing, I also began to discover the various shades of "I miss you."

> *I miss you, damn it. DAMN IT.*
> *I miss you, please come back.*
> *I miss you; you hurt me.*
> *I miss you; I'm losing my mind.*
> *I miss you; what were you thinking?!*
> *I miss you; I'm sorry.*
> *I miss you; why didn't you just stab me in the heart?*
> *I miss you: I'll be nice if you give me a second chance.*
> *I miss you; where are you?*
> *I miss you.*

And there it came, forcing its way up like lava from a volcano, every emotion and every hurt. A visceral and ancient voice began speaking from within me. I marveled at how utterly self-possessed and 'other' it seemed. I continued singing "I miss you" until the musical tracks ended. My last "I miss you" managed to make its way through tears that sounded like a wounded animal crying. To this day, if I ever listen to that recording, I am moved by the purity, conviction and wounded-ness in the voice.

I finished the CD, listening to it at night before going to sleep, hearing my emotions saturating the evocative strains as they swirled and tumbled around me.

The inside jacket of the CD read:

> *Because of the deeply personal nature of this recording, I originally thought not to release it. That it would be*

my closure; my healing; my pain and my joy. But, in the final stages of completing The Girl Beyond the Waves, I came to believe that even the most deeply personal experience is also the most truly universal experience. And, that there is a healing in the sharing... for everyone.

All of us have sustained a loss. It comes in many forms. Loss of innocence; loss of youth; loss of a job. And so, with the untimely and sudden death of my partner in marriage, Maya, I offer this musical chronicle of these emotions...deeply felt.

And that chapter, that part of my healing journey, was put away. I had musically journeyed through the many twists and turns of a loss. And I was glad I had. I had started to purge my grief as, seemingly, ancient as time itself. And I had done it the way I saw fit.

CHAPTER 9

Looking Back
Written August, 2001

It has been over 7 1/2 years since Maya died.

In the past seven years, the physical movement in my life has come to a grinding halt. I have stopped my busy-ness. I've looked at the fascinating ways in which I have been held hostage by, and been made a slave to, my self-image. I've been shown that my needs are interwoven with my personality's construction, that my personality is merely something I have engineered and contrived to keep me safe. I'm not sure I would have noticed these things had it not been for the defining event that systematically tore down the perception I had of who I am. It also brought greater clarity to the events happening around me and my relationship to them.

I would guess that Maya and I were attracted to each other because we had devised a similar strategy for coping with our childhoods. As hyper-vigilant children, we probably improvised two distinctly different selves. One self did what it needed to do to fit in socially; the other was a private, protected self that seemed to operate independently of any social convention. The two were often at odds with each other. One might even resent the other. The two selves took turns being in control.

We recognized this contrivance in the other and it felt familiar. Finally, this familiarity felt like love. Actually, it was one of many misconceptions that needed to be blown apart, for it was this split, this ambivalence, that needed to be one again. As the entire construction was destroyed, so too was the schism. Needless to say, it was not pleasant. It was like losing a partner or having one's wheelchair pulled out from underneath.

The loss of Maya was a very difficult passage, but much of the most difficult work had to do with what the loss triggered, and that is where the blessing is. That is where the *invitation* presented itself to look at what had been blown apart and ultimately to decide, did I want to repackage this "self" or choose to leave it unassembled? For a brief time, I repackaged. Because one can never go back, I saw that it could only be allowed to fall apart again.

And that is where I am now. I do not have the same kind of goals anymore. I am not driven in the same way I was. My priorities are ordered more along the lines of:

What if this was my last day on earth? How would that change the way I love? How would that change the choices I make? Where is the fun?

Dolphins

A lot of this reminder came, interestingly, from dolphins. I had the unique opportunity to swim with dolphins in the wild on many occasions after the loss. The magnificent underwater universe reveals itself as an infinite blue space. The sound of my own breathing, through a snorkel, and the warm water's gentle embrace are my only awareness as I glide through the water. My breath. The phenomenon that is the breath. Through my mask, the sun in the water dances luminous streaks into the deep blue, converging at a point unseen far below.

Then I hear high-pitched squeaks, clicks, and what can only be laughter. I lift my head from the water and, through my mask, I see dozens of dorsal fins glinting in the sun as they stitch through the water's surface. Now and again, one of the Spinner dolphins twirls in the air. My heart races. The closer I swim, the louder the chatter becomes. And then suddenly, like a picture slowly appearing in developer solution, these beautiful creatures appear everywhere. They are playing. They swim deep along the bottom, alongside, underneath and everywhere. The copulation and foreplay and chasing and laughing are endless and seem an expression of pure and utter celebration. We mimic each other. I laugh aloud as we play. They seem to laugh back, noticing my amusement.

I pull out one of the leaves I'd tucked into my swimsuit before getting in the water. I advertise it, humming the theme music to Rocky and Bullwinkle through my snorkel. We take turns chasing the leaf as they chatter excitedly. They watch with bemused curiosity as I allow myself to believe that I can beat them at their game. One of them draws me away from the pod and we chase each other like children as we twist and turn and somersault. Another dolphin drops a leaf for me to retrieve that is just deeper than my comfort level and watches to see if I dive for it anyway.

I watch as the pod disappears into the infinite of blue space. He turns one last time to see if I dare swim to that depth to retrieve the leaf now enticing me as it shimmers gold somewhere near where the shafts of sunlight converge. I grin as he suddenly disappears.

I swear I've re-visited that same dolphin many times since.

But perhaps more than the startling familiarity of that incredible eye as it stared at my soul through the window of my eye, the sound the dolphins made had eternity scripted in it for me. It was a sound that went through me in such a way as to remind me that this body is not of dense flesh and bone. Rather, this body is made up of particles of light held together by a kind of cosmic glue. This memory of the penetrating dolphin sound is with me always. In my mind's eye, forever, I will see that dolphin swimming away with his pod, turning his head every so often to check and see if I had gone down there to get the leaf he had left for me.

When the dolphins were not sleeping or eating, they'd be making love and playing. Like tree squirrels or baby pygmy goats, they are always looking for where the fun is. What can they investigate and have fun with next? The child-like simplicity of this lifestyle spoke grandly to me. That dolphins are at least as intelligent as humans is incontrovertible. That they are far more intelligent is likely. Yet they choose play. They choose simple. They seem to celebrate the eternity of all life and of all living. That eternity does not exist on the horizon of endless time and expanse; it lies hidden where most of us would never think to look: in the moment.

§

Perhaps perversely, I long for the awareness I had in the months following Maya's passing. In those months, the seams of all my beliefs unraveled and illumined a landscape whose only God was the moment. All aspects of past, present, future, the dead, the living, the unborn swam together in one very living and amorphous soup. And death? I had zero fear of death. I could have walked through death's porthole at ANY time.

After Maya's passing, if I was uncomfortable in a situation or social gathering, I simply removed myself from the scene. If I felt something, I inspected it with curiosity and if I was in the company of others, I very simply stated what I felt. If I felt like crying, I let myself cry fully. The people I loved knew it. I told them I loved them. I told them EVERY time I saw them. My passion was fully awake.

Then what is it about today that keeps me from living every day, every moment of my life as if I were about to take my last breath? Have I resumed living "normally" in this attenuated version of living—where my passion, rawness and simplicity has taken a back seat to the mundane? Where has the passion disappeared to that was so very alive when I was in the very vulnerable state following her death?

It's so remarkable to me now, that such an unbearable pain/trauma sponsored this kind of opening. Why does it have to be pain that triggers my awakenings?! Am I in some ways hardly more evolved than a single-celled, primordial speck of consciousness avoiding pain and craving pleasure? But when the pain does come, yeah, when it DOES come – that's when I have an "ah hah!" I would just as soon pain NOT be the only catalyst for change. I'd like to be so keenly aware of my relationship to myself and to my environment that I wouldn't have to be clubbed over the head to make discoveries.

Fish!

When I was in France last year attending a sound and healing workshop, I noticed four children playing around the area where the workshop members ate. It was a Sunday and the grounds were open to the public. The sun shown brightly on this warm summer day on a hill overlooking the French Riviera. One of the children ran to the small cement pond just above where a few of us were sitting and squealed, "Fish!!" As the four-year-old girl looked at the gold fish in the water, the water's surface reflected back to her – her own excited face. The other children ran over and confirmed, "Fish!!"

They looked at the "Fish!!!" with mouths agape for several minutes and then moved on to find fascination, certainly, in something else.

This is what Maya has shown me! Not fish, so much, but she has shone me the wonder of discovery after doing spring cleaning on my personality. I want to take the metallic confetti heart that I stared at on the floor the day after Maya's passing and announce "heart!!" I want to turn that same curiosity into a joyous, celebratory discovery. I want every moment to be "Fish!!"
    Or—Love!!
    Or—Sun!!
    Or—Friend!!
    Or—Music!!

In retrospect, it seems that the profound, though understandable, awkwardness of my friends' behavior around my wife's death speaks to something curious about our culture (or at the very least, about my circle of friends). The attention we lavish on youth, happiness, sex, and power does not leave room for, or even take into account, the existence of sadness in our lives. Death and dying have no room in our perverted addiction with happiness, youth, and vitality. Have we, in fact, grieved the millennia of wars, injustices, subjugations, holocausts, and disease?

We couldn't have. Otherwise something like Princess Diana's death wouldn't have incited such an out-pouring of grief. She seemed to become the projection of everyone's long-suffering and un-grieved grief. Granted, she was a delight to look upon and her public appeal was huge. But the way so many of us were swept up in this global wave of grief would point to something much greater than simply mourning the death of a popular princess. On her death, I feel, we projected the sum of all our little deaths, all our losses, including one of the most vexing of losses – wholeness.

We WERE whole at one time. Weren't we? Somewhere long ago?

The loss of my wife sprang open a Pandora's box of all my unexpressed grief and the attendant suppressed feelings got flung in my face like confetti. Each speck of confetti had its own right to be there and was its own invitation for further investigation. The confetti included anger, depravity, longing, perversion, sadness, emptiness and guilt. Every color of fear was flung in my face wanting to be acknowledged so I could acknowledge the gravity and essence of what had just occurred with the untimely death of my wife. Shit happens. Shit happened to me AND I was clubbed on the head.

My former life was spurious and illusory, even though I tried to be as conscious as I could. At age 17, I had begun a long trek into journal entries which reflected two-hour-a-day forays into understanding what made me tick. I recorded my solitary years vagabonding in Europe and Asia—not only the varied landscapes and people, but the elusive terrain of my own psyche, all in the name of getting to the bottom of IT. But I still needed to be…clubbed on the head. Because IT was still eluding me. And the IT is the wonder, discovery and delight of the moment. And granted, it's not all tra-la-la-la-la. It's up and it's down. And it is a miracle.

Even now, I still may hold Maya's death against God. God patiently waits as I rant and rave. If anything, it is the abiding patience that inexorably wins me over. How can ANY thing be THAT loving and accepting?

I lay myself at the feet of the divine now, humbled by the clubbings, willing to accept and embrace whatever befalls me. I am humbled by what I feel must be the infinite patience of the divine. I am humbled at the beauty and perfection around me. If I simply observe, and not BE my emotions and preconceptions and fears, this life experience becomes a stage where any miracle can happen.

CHAPTER 10

The Sound
Written September, 2001

I've taken my music in an entirely different direction, partially or perhaps even fully due to the influence of this loss. The tremendous solace that I took in listening to R. Carlos Nakai's Native American flute playing every night has instilled a renewed respect and awe in me for music's intrinsic healing power. Particularly, acoustic music, with its myriad harmonics bouncing off each other like an atomic reaction.

Even as a child, lying on the living room floor listening to classical records like Sibelius's *Finlandia* or Humperdinck's *Hansel and Gretel*, I was most certainly being healed. My heart was being healed by these knowing, gentle strains of music. The images springing forth from my six-year-old imagination spread color into the colorless, life into the lifeless. I most certainly owe my "Fish!!!" fascination with music to my earliest exposure to it. And to my parents for having the wisdom to know, somewhere within themselves, that music is important. To these incredibly courageous pioneers of the soul, the composers, I owe my life. (If you happen to be blessed with children, take them to a musical or a classical concert…please…do it for the "Fish!!" of it.)

Intrigued by the notion that all 'stuff' is vibration, that this universe is held together by a kind of cooperative commingling of vibration, would not music be the sweetest expression of vibration? It's creation set to a melody. And, just as vibration destroys, it also creates. There's probably a song in there somewhere.

I can only guess that if my personality hadn't been quite so fixed, Maya's passing wouldn't have affected me as it did. That I would have been able to smile as she passed from one dimension to another is clearly a little extreme. As an emotional, feeling being, I had every right to be attached to Maya. Yet at the risk of sounding too cerebral, if her choice on some level was to leave, who was I to reasonably expect her to stay for me?

Conversations with Maya

During the grieving of the last six years, I'd imagine us, as souls, joking around in heaven. We'd be conjuring up different scenarios in which we could meet each other on earth and force the other to evolve. One of the scenarios went like this:

MAYA'S SOUL

> *OK, OK, I got it…you're in your early 40's, you're single, and you have this beautiful house in the country and…*

MICHAEL'S SOUL

> *…right, I meet you at a dance…*

MAYA'S SOUL

> ...naw, too Hollywood. It'd be better if you were....uh, looking for a housemate because you're wanting to change your life a little...fill it with a little color...make some extra money...shake it up...

MICHAEL'S SOUL

> ...oh, right, RIGHT. And you answer this ad...

MAYA'S SOUL

> ... that I see in the paper that you've put in there for a housemate. So I call you on the phone and I'm, sort of, put off by your manner on the phone...but I come over there anyway...

MICHAEL'S SOUL

> ...and it's love at first sight when you come to the door...

MAYA'S SOUL

> It won't fly. There's gotta be some kind of crescendo or tension...some kind of chemistry thing. A rising action. You know, the slow burn. Besides, all your other lifetimes you've been so...careful...and even distrustful, of women in particular. So, anyway, I come in and you interview me. Gradually, I'm overtaken by this schoolboy charm of yours, even though I thought you were a jerk on the phone, and blam. I move in. We fall in love in the spring. We get married in summer. And I die three months later. All in the same year! Ka-bluie!

BOTH SOULS

> *(hysterical laughter)*
>
> I love it! Yeah. That's great. So perfect.

MICHAEL'S SOUL

But how do you die?

MAYA'S SOUL

Something sudden. Something, uh, dramatic. A CAR crash.

MICHAEL'S SOUL

Great. GREAT. Who thinks of stuff like this?! This is like Shakespeare shit. But, uh, let's not have the blood and body parts thing. You know how I'm squeamish about all that.

MAYA'S SOUL

Done. And because of the suddenness, and all your dashed hopes and dreams, and the way you'll miss me like crazy, it helps you finally figure out what it is to love intimately. Oh sure, you will have been able to love a bunch of people. You'll "love" all your friends. You'll be a huggie, lovie guy. You'll have some girlfriends. You'll think you'll never love again the way you loved me. But then, you'll meet her. This'll be perfect because she will really feel that you have no fear about loving intimately. And you're going to be so grateful to me.

MICHAEL'S SOUL

And your death cracks my heart open SO painfully that I really begin looking at, and re-evaluating, what is truly important in my life…hell, in ANY life.

MAYA'S SOUL

And then you become a healer. You show others what you learned.

MICHAEL'S SOUL

Damn, you're good. What a total crack-up!! That's… that's a good one. A healer. Classic. But what about you? What do YOU get in this scenario?

MAYA'S SOUL

I've got something up my sleeve. I'll let you know….on the NEXT round.

MICHAEL'S SOUL

The next round? But….

(WHOOSHING SOUND – BLINDING LIGHT)

Whaddya mean by the next round…? Hey. What the… Aw, man! That was just getting interesting and here I am in somebody's belly again. Hello? . . . Hello-o? I hope you're planning to take good care of me before I start dividing up into a bunch of cells.

MY MOM

What do you mean you didn't wear anything?

MY DAD

Come on. Quit your worrying. How many times have we done it now and nothing ever happened?

MY MOM

Oh, Abe.

MICHAEL FETUS

Hey, I'm dividing here.

MY DAD

Stop your worryin'..

MY MOM

...but we can't afford....

MICHAEL FETUS

...are you sure you want to do this?..

MY MOM

...a child right now..

Getting to the Core of Healing

Once the door of healing had been flung open, I wanted more.

I wanted to get to the emotional body where the emotional stuff lived, where the ancient, ancestral proclivities handed down from generations before me resided. I reasoned that both cultural information and the details of specific family lineage would be passed on to the fetus through the "melody" of the mother's voice, that within the voice print itself lay all the codified signatures of the family and culture. The music and cadences of the mother's voice became the script and engine that would order the newborn's life.

Making a grand leap, I further reasoned that if I could simulate the amniotic environment and RE-SING my own cultural and family song, I could re-instruct my cellular belief system.

Remembering, too, the powerful impact of the dolphins' sound on my body, I set about looking for a sound bed that would vibrate music and voice as I lay on it. My internet surfing and research placed me at Chuck's doorstep. Chuck had long experimented with sound beds, both the heated waterbed variety and the type that was like a massage table with vibrating transducers underneath. He helped me construct a heated water sound bed. I found it sublimely relaxing to lie on the bed while a deep sustained drone played underneath me (and through me) from a frequency generator.

I recorded CD's that would vibrate my relaxed body into a state of deep receptivity and there...this is where I would try to reprogram my beliefs and my stories.

With music as a backdrop to provide a sustained state of relaxation, I felt guided to record my own voice, speaking gently as a mother would speak to her child. I added the recorded sounds of endlessly lapping waves to suggest the sound of the mother's blood rushing about the fetus. The gentle rocking on the waterbed would simulate the comforting sway of the unborn in the mother's amniotic fluid. I wanted to try and recreate the primal environment where the effects of a mother's words sink into the fetus' tissue. The rise and fall of her voice gently encodes the cultural and familial intelligence in each cell, every developing organ, every bit of cartilaginous mass and sinew.

Through the use of the sound bed, I wanted to massage my cells into a different awareness of themselves. Maybe I could facilitate wiping the cellular memory slate clean so every perception would be a "Fish!!" discovery. It has helped immeasurably. As to whether it's as simple as all that, I doubt it. But it certainly was a powerful tool.

I've begun working regularly with the various ways in which sound and color can be used to effect healing, with myself and clients. As I work, I often hear Maya's voice in the sound and see her sunflower face in the color. But I have not finished grieving. I was told by a bereavement counselor that the grief would come in waves, that as time went on, the waves would have greater and greater separation between them.

When I was in a "broken apart" state, metaphors seemed to present themselves constantly. Every time I was in the sea with waves lapping against my body, I would imagine waves of grief moving through me. They'd rush up to greet me, then flow through me. When watching a river or stream, emotions would flow through and by me. Nothing ever lingered for too long.

If I get into partnership again, I hope I will be able to enter into it with a wholeness I've never brought to a relationship before—a wholeness that would be an invitation to discovery, not an invitation into a relationship based on transactions and need fulfillment.

SECTION TWO

Jennifer's Story
The Gordian Knot of Intimacy

You left me boundaries of pain
Capacious as the sea,
Between eternity and time,
Your consciousness and me.

— Emily Dickinson —

Clockwise from top: Jennifer and Gordon. Galen and Gordon in the garden. Gordon reading in the forest. Galen, young and interior. 1988.

Jennifer's Story: The Gordian Knot of Intimacy

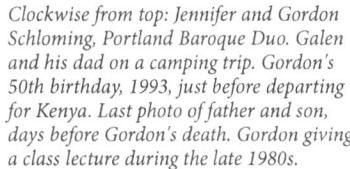

Clockwise from top: Jennifer and Gordon Schloming, Portland Baroque Duo. Galen and his dad on a camping trip. Gordon's 50th birthday, 1993, just before departing for Kenya. Last photo of father and son, days before Gordon's death. Gordon giving a class lecture during the late 1980s.

For 17 years, Gordon's wallet photo.

CHAPTER 1

The beginning...
Or rather, the beginning of the end
December, 2001

How did this happen? (For, like Rilke, we are ill-equipped to answer the why of such things as they come upon us, but perhaps, at least, we can record the simple chronology of the how.)

I was 43 when my husband of 17 years died of prostate cancer. Our young son was eight. A misdiagnosis by his friend and physician resulted in a cancer becoming so advanced that when it was finally revealed, Gordon was given less than two years to live. He was 48. He was dead at 50. At every stage, his dying was an impossible reality to integrate into the meaning of our daily lives. The fact of it abraded breath, chafed all the unregarded sinews of being.

We met over politics. Gordon was a professor of political relations and I was a high level political staffer, both of us passionate about life and our obligation to it. From the beginning, our relationship was far from casual. Even in early courtship, we drove conversation into deep terrain. We aimed at consciousness and played our pairing like a high stakes game. Over the years we accepted the bone-hard work of individual and couples therapy, sanding ourselves down to willing surrender. Our prize? The blessed contradiction of supple union and steely independence. We worked to become graceful and generous in our love.

Our intentions to grow up, to scrabble toward real emotional maturity, served us well when I was diagnosed with multiple sclerosis early in our marriage. I began to suffer vision problems and loss of feeling in my hands during my husband's post-doctoral fellowship year at Princeton University. This assumed a more acute form within months of returning to our home in Portland, Oregon. After the inevitable easy answers failed, my illness was eventually dubbed "possible M.S." I was 28.

I had been in Jungian analysis since the beginning of our marriage, trying to survive the surrender to this new definition as *wife*. My disorientation was flamboyant. In an absent-minded exit from our bedroom, a quick sideways glance through the bathroom door revealed a woman's body in the bathtub. Who was she? With "I do," I had unwittingly stepped into a new and completely unreliable universe. Panicked at being a Mrs., the death into marriage came replete with a corpse, just at the edge of vision. It was a mighty struggle with my own demons, for I had married a vastly capable man and I felt condemned to my own obvious inferiorities by the mere fact of him. He, of course, was not privy to the interior negotiation of worthiness that was being waged in my heart, so the labor of claiming my own deeply grounded personhood was fully my own. This work assumed a new imperative for us both when M.S. entered our lives. The episode of illness lasted about one year, gave a much deeper keel to our relationship, and shaped who I have become.

By the time of Gordon's diagnosis, we had been married 16 years, lived in a number of exotic and demanding third world settings, and raised a precocious six-year-old son. We had traveled throughout Central America to evaluate language programs, lived and concertized in both Peru and Ecuador, and even served as ambassadors to academic conferences in the former Soviet Union. It was a rich life—for although we did not enjoy financial ease, we basked in the best opportunities academia had to offer. And then, with one diagnosis, that world was blown apart.

Responding to a free screening for prostate cancer offered by the neighborhood hospital, Gordon signed up for a PSA test, the standard diagnostic for this type of cancer. Earlier in the year, a strong sense that something was terribly wrong had initiated a visit to his regular physician at our HMO, but the referral he sought was denied. In spite of an impassioned request to be seen by a urologist, his symptoms were laughed aside as the inevitable sad fact of turning 50. Months passed before the unexpected opportunity for the test came in the mail. We were to get the results in about a week.

Expecting news anytime, I was at work in the opera studio when the phone rang. Abandoning the startled singer mid-note, I jumped from the piano and raced to the privacy of a small back study to take the call. Grabbing the phone, anxious to hear the report, I was suddenly captivated by the details of normalcy surrounding me: the shabby orange shag carpet, the fake wood veneer on the walls, the fading wood sash around the window. In a queer assertion of primacy, before any words were spoken, I noticed these things—this ordinariness, the dull ballast of the daily. I wanted the reliable, unregarded substrate, this declaration of the familiar, to cross the telephone wires to me. Listening, I waited for our easy reprieve, the good news. As he began to speak, the receiver in my hand turned to lead. *Cancer.* Like the trip-wire to a bomb, I exploded inside. Losing its mooring, the room spun into suspension, the air thickening into a curious opacity. Time collapsed. Even though I stood with the traitorous phone to my ear, I no longer felt like the true owner of this body. Parts of me had flown to the far edges of the room with Gordon's words, observing the familiar furniture, the fact of it, its very concreteness absurd. How could these things continue to exist, standing motionless and stupid, as my universe was fracturing in the receiver?

> *Prostate cancer is rated by a measure called the Glisan Scale, with designations of 1-10, from least to most aggressive. Gordon had a Glisan 9.*

I have no memory of what I said to my husband. The conversation was very brief, as neither of us had words. No sound we might make could give the air meaning. But now, six years later as I write this, I pray, Oh God I pray, that whatever I said was kind. As we spoke, my legs turned spongy, my disbelieving feet rooted to the floor. I watched legs and feet propping up the rest of me in their odd density, wondering how that all worked—standing up. How did that work?

I willed my disbelieving hands to dial the home of the older of my two brothers. I couldn't return to the piano and singers with this news, alone. When he and his wife answered, their voices, familiar and welcoming tore open the bone of the world and threw it at my feet. Their universe was still firm and good, but mine was suddenly and utterly without foundation. As desperate as I was for the embrace of their love in bearing this news, as soon as they answered, the terrible truth of my solitariness sank in. The damnable diagnosis left me with nothing but the truth to gnaw on. THIS is how it works here. This is how life works.

Silence hung after I first whispered my brother's name, and when the words finally made their way out of my throat, they came dry and hoarse. To speak this, to lend it concrete currency with the telling, was an unthinkable offense. How could I be saying this terrible thing about my husband? And I knew, I knew with this first effort to form words around it, that he was going to die. I haven't admitted that until this moment.

CHAPTER 2

Petitioning Hope...
Sliding Down the Rabbit Hole

The efforts to meet the cancer—the surgery, the radiation, the Lupron—all got their obeisance from my husband, the petitioner. First came the operation, which revealed that the cancer had strayed beyond the margins of the prostate, violating internal organs that were beyond surgering. After a four-hour vigil, heavy with prayer and fear (the impossible and unavoidable mix for many of us) the surgeon met me in the waiting room and said, "The good news is that you've got six to eighteen months to plan. You might get five years if you're lucky." That's what he said. Not, "I am so sorry, this is beyond our means to cure, but not beyond yours to hope—blessings on you both." Not that. Instead, a death sentence.

I hated him, his vast insensitivity, and his appalling stupidity for trampling on the ground of the divine. Nobody could possibly know the outcome of this cancer. There were always exceptions— I was one in some ways myself, in my own encounter with M.S. I answered him with an immediate and furious, albeit silent, "Fuck you." Did he even *know* that his patient had a six-year-old son?

Over the next weeks, Gordon walked on down the medical line-up, trying on drugs and radiation, and renewed psychological work with a Jungian analyst. I was not at all sure how I felt about God.

The first months were buoyed by outrage, which became the engine of hope. It was the crude yet redemptive response to the omnipresent terror that had moved into our lives with the surgeon's decree. Answering the fear, mustering energy and wisdom to meet this challenge, became the ground for all our choices. In the midst of efforts to do all this right, to be big enough to wear cancer, the initial shock finally wore itself into a reluctant surrender to the fact of this disease in our lives. Both of us continued to work full time, claiming the blessed relief of its rhythm. We needed time to walk in smaller shoes, the daily measure, because the soul-sized shoes were too damned big to put on—at least in the beginning. It would take months to be broken apart and stretched by uncertainty before we could fall into this new way of walking.

But if there was a surrender of sorts to the fact of the disease in our lives, there was anything but a surrender to the idea of death. While the cancer was marching through Gordon, I was marshalling a defense against defeat. Stoic (I am a farmer's daughter, there is no other option), I refused to give way to overt and crippling despair, but the ground I stood on was mighty shaky. Carried on a current of unwept tears, the politics of the negotiation slipped off into secret back room bargaining, out of sight of the wisdom I sought. How much of my determination and our courage would be incontrovertible enough to allow Gordon to live? If I grieved this damned disease and really wept, would whoever held the power in this negotiation see me for a faithless cheat, unsure of a Higher Power's unlimited capacity for a miracle? Would I queer the divine mechanism's ability or desire to heal? What if God, or Whoever was behind this whole surreal slip in the world, decided I was failing my measure of valor in this awful assignment—might They judge Gordon accordingly and pass on to some other worthier soul in need of rescue? I did not want any weakness of mine to steal possibility. The equation must be a trade of strength for strength, mustn't it? Wouldn't an even-handed universe work that way?

I LOVE this man. You know that.

He's my breath. You know that.

We've worked HARD at this life business ... Haven't we? You know that, don't You?

My strength for his. Please God.

OH GOD, PLEASE!   PLEASE!!!!!!   ... Please

Of course, none of this dark dealing was visible to inspection. Subterranean certainties about divinity and the weave of the world run unnoticed, like bodily fluids busily swishing about, background to every moment, unquestioned. These were the all too obvious assumptions about the design of the universe; mysteries decodified deep in the murky depths of the heart and beyond the realm of interrogation. I knew my part—I had to help save this wonderful, irreplaceable man.

But there was an underbelly to this shadow bargaining which was laced with danger. Pleading and despair go hand-in-hand. I was staring down the black hole of nihilism, at risk of being unmade by my own anxiety. What if the outcome, whether Gordon would live or die, could not be begged or bargained? What if my beseeching couldn't stand against the dictates of soul-matters beyond our knowing? But then how could I live with that awful possibility? Isn't the promise of prayer to stake a claim and argue an outcome? Petitioning divinity on my daily inhale of terror, I was afraid of what wearing my embattled faith into the world would mirror back about hope. In this jumbled landscape of my heart, I both did and did not want people's pity. I wanted others to feel our pain with us, but I sure as hell did not want them to mirror it back so successfully that it presumed on our hope. And so, wearing this news into the world became like the first phone call to my brother.

If I didn't give sorrow too loud a voice, then I wouldn't risk hammering this terrible mistake into a fixed place in our lives.

The only hitch with such a carefully contrived and unconscious formula is that it doesn't work. Although I snarled myself into an agreeable knot of ferocity and fear, the tango with the world went on. For all the occasions that I successfully held tears at bay, I was caught in many a misstep where my carefully controlled beat of the moment would suddenly slip out of rhythm with itself and I would fall into a far more deeply tuned reality. And there, I wept, beyond terror. The occasions of this undoing would be the oblique moments, the ones to the side rather than straight ahead, for the insidious break in this carefully constructed emotional dike is the world itself. An exquisite vulnerability overtook me so that all texts and signs of the world, all beauty, all pain, penetrated with deep and immediate clarity.

When death crosses the threshold and stations itself in the corners of one's life, the world begins to answer with absurd splendor. When facing the risk of losing one's place in it, the present moment becomes vibrant. It sings and suffers eloquently in one's ears and eyes and heart, and one feels deeply. And somehow, in the process of reconciling all of it—fear and courage, beauty and loss—we become more than we were.

About six months into treatments, Gordon decided that the chance to lead a student study abroad trip to Kenya offered not only an opportunity to step away from the disease, fearless, but also a welcome chance to mentor in a more personal way than the college classroom normally affords a professor. I didn't know if he was choosing to live or die. Now I realize, and perhaps then I did too, that it was both.

We interviewed students for the trip, picked the hardiest, ran orientations, and got on the plane with six months' worth of medicine for cancer and malaria and 20 boxes of medical supplies for village clinics in Kenya. All 27 kids on this trip knew the choice Gordon was making, and all of us wanted to make some small and healing difference. As it turned out, we were able to help build a clinic in a remote village during the monsoon season. Many of us came down with malaria. Many of us would have done it again without a second thought.

Gordon's strength flagged, and we stayed up late many nights debating whether or not to terminate the trip so he could get home and get help, but the obligation to the kids and the seduction of adventure were enormous.

It is unnerving to admit that I don't know why he did not try to save himself, since a return to the States seemed his only remaining hope. He had a son who mattered more to him than all of this, so why didn't we just pack up and fly home to try alternative therapies? Unless he knew that the cancer was winning, and gutting it out in Africa was choosing to be recklessly alive in the little time he had left. His choice to stay was wrenching. Every moment of living through this experience was knotted: judgments, measures of worth all tangled together. There was no certainty anywhere, except in the reassurance of our embrace. At least we had each other. Like prowling lions at night, fear encircled us and cut our feet on the sharded threshold of each new day.

We returned to the United States on schedule, checked in with doctors, adjusted medications, renewed the counseling and began a move to a new home five hours away in Southern Oregon. We had bought it before the diagnosis, but stayed in Portland for the Kaiser medical coverage. Now that the trip was over and Gordon's fatigue forced a departure from academe, we began the move.

It is hard to believe that Gordon's physicians did not counsel against this after the enormous effort of travel in Kenya. Perhaps they did, or maybe he didn't tell them. Gordon was charting his own course, following a compass pulled hard by the gravity of death.

From a reasoned perspective, the completely reckless embrace of this new adventure is of course beyond the speaking. His passion guided our decision-making. He was eager to make the move and begin the remodel of a new home, so we did. Like staying in Africa, neither of us wanted to admit a limit. We wanted to live as if the disease didn't have a voice in our choices, or a right to limit our freedom. I shared in this hubris. Even though I was terrified of his dying, I wanted to believe in his vitality, his excitement, his eager and capable reach for a future.

In hindsight, the promise of a move, of getting to start over and remake oneself, carries tremendous hope. On some register of value, the rashness of this colossal outlay of vital energy must have made sense. For although it certainly seemed to have hastened his death, he was passionately engaged in the delicious details of the building project, and it left my son and me our new home. How can I judge this? We began the move in June. He was dead in December. It had been 18 months from the beginning of the whole odyssey. Gordon had stepped into the smallest frame of the surgeon's cursed comment.

As I look back on these months now, I cannot find my son except for a few scattered memories of Kenya—snapshots, vivid and generally laced with terror, like the green mamba that slithered across his path a moment behind his gleeful leap for the soccer ball. Memory holds real danger indelibly, but for all the other moments of ordinary fear, there is no trace. I don't know where he was during these long months of his dad's disease. I can see him out of the corner of my eye, but never in the center, in focus. Neither do I know for sure how many friends and family abided with him, holding his hand and his heart during this trial. I know I tried to be attentive and loving, but I have no clear memory of being anyone's mom. All I remember is cancer.

Looking Back IV
June, 2011

Michael: *I'm immediately struck by the huge difference in how our losses were set up. You had these 18 months of bargaining with God. He had 18 months to defiantly declare his vitality in the face of a death sentence from his medical community. Mine came out of the blue.*

It was as if the enormity of the Kenyan trip and the house remodel would marshal new life within him such that he would be larger, and more imposing, than the cancer itself...and if everything went according to the outrageous plan, the cancer would retreat with its tail between its legs. I admire his phenomenal courage to thrust himself into such a physically demanding landscape. And I can't help but feel that if his hearty laugh in the face of death didn't buy him his life back, at the very least he was providing you and Galen something big and beautiful. A forever memorable trip, in spite of the circumstances, and a more livable home. His grandeur humbles me.

I would ask you this:

Were you supporting him in his indomitable showing of spirited renewal or were you biting your lip?

Jennifer: I was barely breathing. Cheerleading on oxygen. Thrilled at the overt danger of lions, hyenas, as trades for the covert terror of death. Grateful to be sweating together over composite shingles on the new *roof as we laid them, rather than squirming in the waiting room during radiation treaments. I now realize that I was fucking terrified. All the time. There was no way I could have admitted that and gotten up in the morning as anyone's wife. I was reaching for a transfusion of hope from any possible source, looking to the remodel, the trip, ANYTHING, that might MAKE THIS GO AWAY.*

CHAPTER 3

The Unthinkable
September, 1994

In September, Gordon made a solo trip to Portland for a check-up, as he had begun to feel new discomfort while we were working on the remodel. I was a little afraid for this trip, but not wildly so, as he had mustered ready stamina for the carpentering and heavy work of home building. He still seemed strong, if in pain.

He called, agitated, on the evening after the appointment just as I was putting Galen to bed, to tell me it was the end; they were giving him days, weeks at best. I sat at the kitchen table writing his words on a legal pad as he spoke, unable to hear or see anything in the room except the odd cast of the lamplight on the page. Curiously steady that light—how could it hold its purpose? I felt only the distant but reliable contact of pen on paper. This thin, inky track was my anchor. Had the table been barren of some means to mark my place, this news, I might have drifted away from time and the night altogether.

He was leaving. Cancer, that bitter, miserable thief, was stealing my love. And whoever was inside my skin holding the receiver seemed to be going too. As I listened, I felt the news cutting out my heart. It was news beyond the bearing. Of course the diagnosis had been morbid, but none of us who knew and loved him, none of us expected him to die. This was the man to beat the odds. I whispered my answer to this news: "Please, please don't tell me anymore. I can't put Galen to bed and bear this too. Come home to me; tell me when we're together." And that began the first of the long nights into his death.

Gordon returned several days later, my cousin chauffeuring his long ride home. As he got out of the car, I raced to meet him and we fell into a desperate embrace –closing out cancer, hanging on in this moment, to life. Death was breathing on us now; never before had our arms held one another so tightly. Anguished, we knew we were losing one another.

New radiation treatments began, more meds, much, much more pain. I called on every healer and herb our community could deliver and Gordon could tolerate. I was utterly incapable of giving up hope. I couldn't surrender and I did not want him to surrender to this damnable disease with its fucking relentless insistence. It was impossible that it might win and get to keep him.

Where was God? Where were the angels or whatever invisible forces out there that heal? WHERE WERE THEY???? What was keeping them??? I simply could not imagine my life without Gordon in it. How would I breathe? Why would I breathe?

His brothers came to visit, his parents came to visit, his friends flew in, and all the family nearby showed up for Thanksgiving. Gordon called on stamina from God knows where, settling his now thoroughly ravaged body onto the floor for the holiday, where he could play with his son and young nieces and nephews. He spent the day fully engaged as father and uncle and died 10 days later. It was his final gift to us all.

With the sort-of exception of Thanksgiving (when I don't

remember really seeing him—only his dad), I don't know what became of Galen after this September call. This was his first year at a new school, in the first weeks of the school year—and his dad was dying. Surely I made school lunches, shopped, cooked and cleaned for us, registered the school day as a claim on my world. These things happened. But when I look for them, time washes gray. I must have talked about homework, didn't I? I must have talked about death, didn't I? But I don't remember it. On the day of his dad's death, he must have been overnight with my parents, wrapped in the safety of family somewhere—I guess. Did I even see him that day?

Gordon awakened on December 5th, as usual (although what was usual these days?), turned to face me, and said, "It's time, Jen. I've got to go." Utter calm. Clear, certain, unwavering. No petitioning for any more minutes. It was time to give up the fight. Until that moment, I had not been able to concede that he was really dying. I had maintained a dogged hope for a miracle all the impossible way through these months, days, hours, until now. As soon as he said it, however, time and purpose telescoped into a different resolve, and that was to end well. No more battling, no fear, no grief. Simply ending honorably, awake to one another, recognizing who we each were and what we had created in this love together, that was all.

I must have wept some (how could I not?), but I don't remember it, for the decision was inviolate. There was no other now. We forgave one another for everything, even the dying. (A promise I have not kept well, I'm ashamed to admit.) I told him I loved him and was with him, and that we would play this to the finish together, even though I knew full well that like all of his suffering with this illness, the dying belonged to him alone. For the next 18 hours he set about the business of letting go, working to release his body from this life.

It was snowing outside, the remodel wasn't fully closed in, and like the interpenetrating world of our unfinished house and the snowy outdoors, worlds in our bedroom opened into one another as the hours passed. His face would change expression, looking eagerly toward something or someone I couldn't see. Other times his expression bore such pain it was excruciating to witness, except that in the suffering, it had become luminous. It felt like an enormous otherness was claiming him, for his anguished body began to shine with opalescent radiance. We talked very little because it was obvious that this process of relinquishing flesh was taking all his energy. Every bit of it. It had been an athlete's body before the cancer, sturdy and strong, and it was an enormous vitality to release, even ravaged by disease. It was taking all his strength to die; he looked and felt like someone in labor.

The hospice nurse showed up mid-morning to apply the morphine pump (did I call her? how did she get there?) and it did not go well. She seemed clumsy, unaware of the refined field he had already reached in his effort to exit. There was an exquisite fineness about him as his body spun its energy ever lighter. She plowed straight into it as she struggled to get the damned thing attached. I hated her density, her fumbling hands and out-of-tune heart. I hated that my husband was dying. Of course she meant well, but she was botching it and I couldn't help. How in the hell could it be that the supposed answer to pain came with pain? I was polite and miserable.

And yet, whatever her efforts, my judgments about them could not coexist with the world Gordon was creating in this room. Dying will not brook untruth or smallness in its field. Without my choosing it, I was cracked open, broken into forgiveness. There was no other feeling possible. For my husband dying, for the nurse blowing it. . . . So much letting go.

My cousin, Maryl, who had recently shepherded her stepson's dying, arrived unannounced from her business three hours away. She said Doug (her deceased stepson) had told her Gordon was going, and it was time to help. She had simply left her desk and started the drive south. Time and space were swimming into whole new contexts in my bedroom, so I did not have any sense to wonder how that could be. I don't know that we said more than a word to one another. She watched for a moment as the nurse struggled with the pump, then immediately dialed Judith, her closest friend from Doug's last days and the head of the Kaiser hospice team in San Francisco. The two of them took over. I trusted that Gordon was in the care of people who knew and loved him now, and that this damned world of meds that I knew nothing about would no longer work against him but on his behalf. As for Maryl and Judith—there are no words. How is it that some people know exactly the right things to do in times like these?

As evening approached, another cousin arrived with a Christmas tree, stand, and lights. I had no idea he was coming. There was an urgency about his mission, a need to give this last gift. He busied himself with setting it up in the living room, getting it just so, at a distance from Gordon's deathbed but close enough to stake his intention to be here and express his love. I think he was calling on the hope of this symbol to carry Gordon to a right end, to offer this last blessing of a promise of Christmas, of the promise of a Christ. I don't imagine that he had this in mind as much as in heart—he just had to give this gift. Gordon was not a practicing Christian and I am Jewish, so the tender urgency of his gift was all the more touching. I think he was trying to save Gordon. But maybe I'm wrong. Maybe he was just trying to love him, to say one last thank you in a gift conjuring both beauty and hope. It was a surprising generosity, the insistent affirmation of life in the middle of death.

My two brothers arrived from Portland just as the tree was

asserting its place in this scene, having driven a hard six hours to say good-bye. The three men greeted the terrible gravity of their coming together by breaking out Christmas beers. What else was there to do? I was in the bedroom with my husband dying, and these guys were in the kitchen trading football scores. How could the space of a few square feet in this house hold two such disparate realities? Gordon heard them and got out of bed (where did he find the strength for that?), cracked a joke about beers and Ensure (his only food for days), and toasted them with an empty can. He loved them, they knew it, and he left them laughing. It was his last act. He went back to bed, and several hours later, he was dead.

It is a Jewish tradition to read Psalms during dying and to time a recitation of the central affirmation of faith (Shema Israel, Adonai eloheynu, Adonai echad) with the last breath. I had been sitting with Gordon, filling the desperate intimacy of this quiet together with prayers, with impassioned cheerleading about his ability to do this last act well.

I believe in you. I always have.

I love you, and oh, it seems I always have.

Over and over and over. Could there ever be too many times to say it?

Galen and I will make it. We'll be all right.

It is okay to leave. You've done this life well.

Wonderfully well. Remarkably, magnificently, courageously well.

We'll be all right.

I love you. I always will.

It was my mantra of farewell. And for all that my brothers and cousins were about, I did not factor them into my world—I didn't want to. I just wanted to be alone with Gordon, utterly alone. Anything other than his breath was a terrible distraction.

I had been so busy with prayers and blessings, so focused on doing this right and loving large enough to help carry him into whatever awaited him, that his last breath made sense. I knew he had been born into something else, that these hours had been a birth not a death, and that something deeper and truer than I could touch had remained alive. The body was cold and still, but I knew that who he was continued out of sight, called elsewhere. It was palpable, this purposiveness in his leaving. The last breath was a willing surrender and a greeting both. There was newness on the other side of it, and I felt it.

Enduring the long hours of this vigil, I had worn myself into a kind of readiness as well. Unaware of the effort, I had labored toward this transition with him. And, oh God, I was so lucky. Weary into a sublime exhaustion, relieved, uncertain of my next step, and lucky. Lucky to have had this time to say good-bye. Lucky.

CHAPTER 4

And Now, Fucking Unbelievable SILENCE

How could it possibly be this quiet? The end of a voice—the real goddamned end. Except that it isn't. Except that it is. Sort of. And it doesn't seem that damned at all, except for those of us left with "all of that love and nowhere to put it." (Galen's words.)

My father, who lives a mile away on a hill overlooking our house, had awakened in the middle of the night, at the time Gordon was dying. He had felt compelled to step out onto his deck, where he witnessed Gordon departing with a heavenly escort.

As a farmer, Dad's language has been framed within the concrete world of machines and dirt his whole life, so angels were a fantastic claim to truth. But he saw them, and perhaps because of this extreme and sacred otherness that marked the night, there was no questioning my desire to have Galen return home the next morning. I wanted him to see his dad's body on the bed, to see the struggle finished, to have the chance for one last goodbye before the undertakers came. It seemed terribly important for him to be in the presence of death, to be with me and know its feel, its unavoidable correctness.

Galen entered the room, remarkably calm. The worst had happened. What was left to fear? There was nothing for either of us to do but face it, eyes open. I told him that I had chanted prayers all through the night, telling his dad how much I loved him, trying to knit my love into the divine fold of his father's leaving. I told Galen that if there was anything he wanted to say or do, his dad would surely feel it. Galen took this in, looked at me and at his father, walked to the foot of the bed and sang a good-bye song to him—an extremely focused, clear and beautiful good-bye.

Neither of us can remember now which song it was; it is beyond reach, locked inside the sacred stillness of those first hushed hours after his father's death. Failing its name, memory holds that it was a song his father had loved—important, strong, and unquestionably a benediction. Galen blessed his dad's leaving. As I write this now, the memory of his courage brings me to tears. He was barely eight years old—where did he find the strength to stand in the center of death's sacred hoop and sing?

The rabbi conducted a service for our family at the funeral home where Gordon was to be cremated. He had received ritual washing by members of the Hevra Kadisha, a volunteer organization from within the synagogue that assumes the sacred task of blessing the body before burial (or in our case, cremation). The team recites prayers that call to the being who was and continues to be in time and space we cannot fathom. Once these prayers of thanksgiving and release have been said, the body can be surrendered.

I stood next to the simple pine box, studying the flickering glass candle bearing the Star of David on its lid, feeling without means to face the crowd or this odd box that stood for Gordon. All I could see was the candlewick burning away, screaming in its terrible silence that its disappearing light meant my husband had vanished. The candle and I knew its purpose. The words of the service fell into the air around me with as much substance as the wick's wispy smoke. Sounds that surely meant something filigreed the room, but I hadn't the means to follow them. The distressing angles of this box, so starkly matter-of-fact and un-alive, stiffened me as well. Without softness or breath, the inert and awful fact of this box as my companion, as the thing that replaced my husband as the locus of relationship, left me struggling with my own breathing fleshiness—with the unsettling continuity of my very aliveness. As the service went on, I stood stroking, patting, loving the box—reaching for the life, for my love and my ground that were contained within it—wanting for this thing under my hand to live somehow. Oh, that wood!—it had no idea what it held!

We exited the funeral home as a group, following attendants to the incinerator outside. It had not dawned on me that cremation was the close of the service, and that when the words were done, the only thing left was to witness the end. Now I understood the unbreathing purpose of the box, for the woman walking in my shoes these last steps to the incinerator turned wooden as well—she could neither see nor feel anything but the imperative to finish this trajectory.

I had no other purpose than to soldier behind Gordon's simple box, partnering it to its last station; to finish this, to play it out, a wide-awake witness to my beloved's demise. And when we arrived at ground zero, the target of all this courage, I stood facing a disinterested concrete block furnace, a dully efficient piece of business—a construction utterly unresponsive to my heart and the portion about to be stolen. The asphalted, concrete ordinariness of this site, its plain ugliness, seemed a theft—a betrayal. How could it be that my life with Gordon was going to end here? Was there to be no beauty, no gracefulness surrounding the return of flesh's gift to ash? This was mere disposal, crude and workmanlike—the sacred given over to the wretchedly profane. It felt woefully insensitive to a larger realm of meaning, crass, and somehow deeply wrong. And, like his death, it was unstoppable.

When they opened the oven doors, my arms took flight—a silent scream to the heavens—reaching of their own volition up over my head, an involuntary reflex, both prayer and surrender to the utter awfulness of this. As they pushed him in, my heart followed, and everything burned and turned to ash.

As the doors closed on my beloved husband, my back registered an exodus behind me. Galen was surrounded by his uncles, a small figure stranded, bewildered on the asphalt in front of the furnace. They detoured him to the beautiful old cemetery across the street, trying to save their little nephew from drowning in a context so damnably bleak. I learned later that they had gone to address the gravestones, to enfold him in another kind of death—the one in a green and verdant place. Trading fire for trees, despair for hope. I wish I could say that I had thought to protect Galen in this way, but I had lost track of him completely in these last moments. I have learned only in this writing that he was standing at the back, his hand in a friend's as he watched his dad be cremated. I hope the friend was there because I thought to ask someone to be with Galen, to shield him from the shock of this last vision. But I am not sure. Maybe someone simply made that decision for me, grabbing onto the pathetic hope that our bodies in front of his, our mulish and stupid density, could protect him from any of this awfulness.

Now, I wish I knew. I wish I *knew* that I was trying to protect my son. How in the hell could I not know this for sure? How could I have been so disoriented by my own blistering determination to march onward and finish this honorably that I lost sight of my own son? Can this be forgiven? How could I not know?

The formal services took place over the next few days, the public farewells with old and new family and friends. I see now that we were wrapped in the wings of a centrally abiding love: Galen and I were unobtrusively shepherded through each next step of these initial details of death. I needed to feel like I was still in charge of my world, that I had a role I was fulfilling that was worthy and correct. As I stumbled through the hours, determined to do this piece of death with consummate courage and grace, those about me protected this crumbling sense of dignity. My false and fragile authority was never violated.

How many mourners are spared the galling certainty of those who claim to know the divine rationale for their loss, or the boomerang of good intentions that manifest as manipulation of their affairs, affirming that they are not capable of coping? I suspect very few. But no one, not one person in our lives said that Gordon's death was for the best, or wondered how in the world I would ever make it. They gave me my place in this excruciatingly vulnerable time, and they left hope unscratched, protecting a future I couldn't see but that was shielded from harm, undiminished by withering, unconscious comments.

As I look back now, however, I realize that each act I executed was fueled by a dangerous mix of grace and adrenalin. Shock's numbing strength has limited mileage. In those first shaky days, family stepped forward and took the helm. They fed us, entertained Galen while putting pen and paper in my hand to write the obituary, outlined the details of who needed to be contacted in order to set up services, and somehow managed to leave me thinking that I was doing all these things.

I was unaware that they were all keeping the earth from faulting under my feet. Like midwives, two cousins attended a shopping sortie with me, escorting a manic mission to find the magic cloak that would let me slide through the dangers of these memorial services, invisible. They thought they were fielding panic about a new dress. Even though I had a wardrobe of black performance attire as a professional musician, nothing with any history to it could step up to the unparalleled gravity of this moment.

In hindsight, I suspect I just felt unable to step into any article of clothing that I already owned. I could not go through the public testaments to Gordon's death in a costume that had felt his eye, known his presence. I raced to find the blackest damned dress on the rack; it was the only color that spoke the truth of how hollow I felt; erased from substance, erased from meaning. How much black would be enough to shield me, to anchor my flimsy mooring during these services? Any unregarded moment risked pulling the curtain back on all that terrifying pain and the awful possibility that it would swallow me. Time had stopped with Gordon's death. Like an old tin can, I felt metallic and empty. I *had* to have this clothing to hide in, this protection from a world I was afraid might get too close and discover I was not there.

My synagogue provides small black ribbons that grieving family members can pin on and tear to mark their loss. They were passed out and we tore them. Little, tiny magic cloaks. I knew I was supposed to feel both protected and relieved by this gesture, and I was dutifully grateful for the attempt to register empathy, but my disrespectful heart screamed betrayal. I felt like I'd been offered a micro-bit of truth when the occasion demanded the whole of it. As much as the symbol aims at a real emotional mark, the means seemed ludicrous. The universe had just torn itself into meaninglessness; how could a tiny ribbon even presume to approximate the scope of this loss?? I needed a swath of cloth and I needed to rip the shit out of it. Instead, my heart was supposed to fit in the minimal space of a few threads—sanitized sorrow titrated to a convenient measure. Had they ever *met* Gordon? Why in hell would anyone think this was enough? I know that it is to the community's credit that this symbol exists at all, but to believe that a few inches of ribbon can possibly stand as a worthy substitute for tearing one's shirt is absurd.

As I write this, however, I realize that hindsight must concede the matter. Some pain gets symbolic acknowledgement because NO measure of ANY size can even begin to speak its truth. Too small was not the synagogue's fault. It wasn't anyone's fault.

I wanted so desperately to be found, and God, I was so lost. Even the damned symbols didn't throw me a line. Nothing was big enough to register the size of the hole in my heart.

In fact, this community *didn't* know Gordon. Nor did it know how closely matched we were as a team. We had loved and respected one another in an unusually deep way—one that people felt and were drawn to. We had talked our world into being together, sharing it all, and now with his death, I did not know who I was. The generosity of a new community that gathered with Galen and me in the polite formalities of concern did the best it could by me. I know that. But with the exception of my parents and visiting family and friends, these earnest strangers didn't know who I had been before I wasn't that anymore. The only map I had for myself had lost its reference point, and there was no mirror to help remember me to myself. For all my gritty resolve to do this courageously and well, I was *lost*. I walked through the steps of these services a profoundly bewildered initiate—new to this place, new to widowhood. No wonder I was panicked about a dress to hide in. . . I had no idea anymore who was putting it on.

Because Galen's class had tracked his dad's dying, they came to the local memorial service. I put the box of ashes on the podium before them, and Galen and I talked about death. I have no memory of what we said, except that I suspect it was ballsy and direct. We were still in shock and fueled by that strange strength that overtakes one when faced with the unimaginable. We had seen countless animal carcasses in Africa—the plains were littered with wildebeests, zebras, cats, even hyenas that had died in the drought on the Serengeti. Death had become an indelible impression. When Galen asked me about cremating his dad, I simply said we needed to do that because there were no lions here to eat the body. In Oregon, we managed death this way. It was sufficient. He got it. *Really* got it. So, we could talk about death and be unafraid of ashes because his dad had given us this last trip, this last odd and magnificent adventure. It became the only real and almost large enough frame for comprehending his dad's death: we both knew that all creatures die. His father SHOULDN'T HAVE, but we couldn't act like we didn't know the truth about death. It's impossible to imagine how we would have gotten through this without Africa behind us. It's the only piece that made it make any sense at all. The only one.

We not only received community attention in the first days around Gordon's death—flowers and remembrances from his many colleagues, but I chose to sit shiva as well. For a week we held services of remembrance in our home, telling stories on Gordon, laughing, crying, holding him near. Galen disappeared for these. My medicine was his poison.

At the end of the last gathering, several close women friends escorted me out the front door into the night, walking with me along the roadside a fair distance from the house. On our return, I was surprised when they stood to the side, waiting for me to enter alone. I had the sudden and awful realization what this meant. They stood as witnesses to the unavoidable fact that when I crossed the threshold *this* time, and into the days ahead, I would do so alone. Shiva was over, and I am no longer who I was. It is an unspeakably lonely ritual—bleak, powerful, inescapably true.

But these were the public things. How we each were doing privately is another matter. In the second week, we fell out of the close embrace of family and friends who needed to reclaim their own lives. Galen and I entered the astonishing enormity of the new and suffocating silence in our house. It was awful beyond the speaking. It felt like the air had been sucked out of this space, our lives, and neither of us knew how to breathe anymore. I know people left food for us, I know we ate—we must have. I know we slept some, and I know that I tried to get Galen to school. We were always late and the teacher was often distressed at the disruption to her class, but I was WAY beyond caring about her class. How could she possibly think that showing up late to her class mattered? This outside measure of our reality was utterly at odds with the effort it was taking merely to be, let alone do. Galen and I were trying to survive. She didn't understand the stakes. I didn't have the energy to explain.

The house was in chaos because construction had stopped when Gordon's attention had shifted to the work of dying. During the last days, when he had too little strength to leave the bed, I had been ploughing on, trying to paint, lay flooring, determined to get the damned thing finished so he (we) could rest. It was all too much, way too much, but there was no way out I could see but to try and finish it. I suspect now that I was playing out a second agenda in this ferocious labor, and that was a misguided, essential (I thought), last-ditch effort to make things come round right. To fix what God was not—to finish the house and heal the man—all the while racing, breathless, from my own fear.

I didn't make it. When Gordon died, the house wasn't even fully enclosed, and it was the dead of winter. Galen and I had to deal with this. We lived out of boxes, in an unfinished home, in a community that was new to us.

Families from Galen's school and the synagogue came to help smooth down the rawest edges of our construction mess so that the house would at least have heat and be livable, earnest faces moving through our space ordering what I could not. Some of those faces I remember, many I have lost beyond the margins of memory. There are no doubt people in this community who helped put us together in those first blind days after Gordon's death, folks that I pass in grocery stores and on the street, whom I fail to register. I have no reference for individual acts of extraordinary kindness—memory will not hold more than the fact of this help; its form has become a blur. Whatever gratitude found voice at the time was the best I had. It is all I had. But now I wish I knew. I wish I could look each person in the eye and say thank-you. Thank-you for helping keep us alive.

We lived out of boxes for the next two years because once everyone left, I couldn't do it. Fully unpacking, putting the house to rights and creating order out of chaos was an impossible assignment. The demands of working and caring for Galen took all the strength I had. How could I possibly get the blasted boxes unpacked when I couldn't muster interest in this home? Why would I want to inhabit this unfinished dream without my beloved? I didn't care—I did not feel obligated to even try. The adrenalin had spent itself. How did Galen survive with a mother who felt like this? Oh my God, how did he do it? The air in our house was thick with weariness.

Nights slipped their rhythm completely, so that I began waking at 3:00 a.m., reeling in the rest of the night on the long line of semi-awake consciousness. Boundaries between night and day dissolved, and hours swam into one another without my seeming to have inhabited them. I did not know where I was. I don't remember whether Galen was sleeping much or not in the beginning, but surely if it was this slippery for me, he had to have been suffering as well. We would lift out of it at the earliest hour we could manage, drive the too-damned-long drive to school, and I would leave him to meet the world on his own.

It did not take long before his nights became regularly haunted by nightmares. One afternoon he took a swing at a girl on the playground, and the teacher, who now had a fairly clear fix on us as a family, invited him to stay outside with the hay bales and have at it. She would be at his side and he could just let fly. I will never forget her insight and compassion for Galen on this terrible day, for he was confused and frightened by what he had done. Like his mom, he had lost the comfort of an easy rapport with whoever was inhabiting his body—the whole business of being was pretty damned unfamiliar.

We checked in with a highly recommended children's counselor, and after a very few visits, she determined that Galen was actually way ahead of any curve on grieving, and he would make it. She didn't need to see him anymore. Galen gratefully agreed with that assessment and we stopped. I was more than a little surprised, and far from comforted by her confident assessment. How could his misery be way ahead of the curve? *What* curve? Certainly his pain could not be called success, but I didn't know what else to offer him, as we both had decided that we couldn't join an organized group on grieving. We were both desperately private, and, I suspect, too scared to cross the threshold of public grieving. But as a result of this introversion, we were without a surround of others suffering our same madness. Galen was isolated at school, unable to meet other kids' eyes, let alone speak to them, and not one of them had a clue how he felt or how to reach out to him. Not one. The only one who could guess at his misery was his fully overwhelmed mom. And so, we persevered.

Looking Back V
June, 2011

Michael: *I marvel at the beyond-his-years knowing that Galen had in the face of such a disassembled reality. How he seemed to know what was right for him:*

Having the presence of mind and grounding to sing the song at the foot of his father's death bed when moments before his life had been shattered.

He knew, deeply, that pouring over memories of his dad while sitting shiva with friends was not right for him.

He knew that he needed to let loose on the hay bales.

What did you make of Galen's self-possession during this time when the "air was sucked out" of your house and your hearts had been flattened by the erasure of a life?

Jennifer: *I remember being moved and worried both. His coping came at the cost of eye contact with any of us. Which meant, no doubt, that the effort to dam the terrifying enormity of those feelings took all his strength. I am certain my sorrow scared the hell out of him, and he spent a lot of time checking to see if I was OK. Like me, he had gone into high alert, and he was tending what remained of his former life with as much vigilance as he could muster.*

The air we breathed was so thick with bewilderment that talking, let alone moving through the spaces of our home, was like trying to swim through snow drifts. It is hard to imagine how he navigated all of this without becoming an exceedingly strange little kid. He had every right to implode. He didn't. So, I guess the direct answer to your question: I believed he was able to persevere because his dad was helping him. I was asking for Gordon's help with Galen all the time, and I felt certain he was there. I was counting on it, since my former capability seemed to be drifting out of reach.

I remember it wasn't just the silence—it was the weight of the silence. The effort to move in any direction was enormous. Staring out the front window on legs made wooden by confusion, hobbled by overwhelming soul-fatigue, such that choosing left or right required too much of a decision. My ability to communicate safety for my child? Sketchy. Very sketchy.

CHAPTER 5

The First Six Months—M.I.A.

Timeless time, no time, colliding worlds, surfing. Taking the next step—just taking it...Gorecki.

One of the two cousins who took me shopping for the non-negotiable funeral dress (the one who had chauffeured Gordon home) brought me a stack of yellow legal pads and a new package of pens. It was her departing gift to me before her return to Portland. There is no way she could have known that it was pen on paper that had provided ballast during Gordon's call from Portland with the last terrible news. And even though at that time (could it only have been three months earlier?) it had been the inky miracle of rendering a trace as the world dissolved that made pen and paper crucial, my assignment for these days, weeks, months after his death, was maybe no different. I needed some means to leave a mark and know that I still was. I did not understand the curious imperative she felt about my needing to have these supplies on hand. I didn't have an inkling what they might mean; how could she? But she is Maryl's sister, so maybe large knowing comes in families.

For many of the standing and staring hours that I spent, some passed with pen in hand. Generally I wrote on scraps of old envelopes not yet recycled, now lost in bottoms of drawers or thrown away. Somehow the commitment to a whole legal pad seemed too considered a fix on this friable reality. But I wrote. And I knew that someone who loved me was hoping and expecting that I would. It has taken six years to enlist that gift into service, but finally there are legal pads spread throughout the house. I feel more alive because of it. Their yellow litter makes me happy.

Music began to play a bigger role in my life now as well. Although Gordon and I had performed professionally as a baroque duo (he on recorder, me on harpsichord), and even though we owned a wonderful library of tapes and CD's, since returning from Africa and beginning the move, the music had stopped. I have come to think that this absence of essential beauty, of music, played a part in Gordon's death. We had both breathed and loved our worlds into being through music, yet in the excitement of moving and remodeling, without noticing what we were doing, we forgot it. I now believe that he needed this music: for joy, for sorrow, for his very spirit and vitality.

As Dr. Oliver Sacks so elegantly observed in his book, *A Leg to Stand On*, music can play an astonishing role in organizing the body's ability to heal. He writes not only about his own experience with a badly broken leg, but also about a number of his patients who shared kindred leaps in recovery when they listened to music they loved. It seems very likely to me that Gordon became "unmusicked." I count it a fateful unconsciousness on our part, an unthinking and far more costly subtraction than I can even pretend to guess.

And now in these first weeks after his death, I returned to it. A single work had carried me through his illness and it was the one that I craved now: Henryk Gorecki's Symphony # 3, composed in 1976 as a requiem to his Polish homeland. It begins with an extremely long, slow lament from the double basses, at first barely audible, that moves through the three movements into undulating swells of the whole orchestra, with a soprano soloist crying the truth of unspeakable pain in a simple, plaintive lyric over it all. It remains minor until the last few bars, and it speaks to me of enduring. Of unrelenting suffering that must be born—there is no other choice. And in the bearing, there is transformation.

I had first heard the symphony when a brand new recording of it was being featured on NPR, just weeks after Gordon's diagnosis. I was driving to work, and in the first measures of the piece, I knew I was in trouble. Weeping, I looked for a place to pull over. This music knew what words could not tell about how cancer felt in our lives. I gave it to all the family, played it throughout the illness, and now returned to it after his death. I lived in it for the first two years of widowhood. Nowhere else was I so fully found, in both my sorrow and determination to survive, as I was in this music.

But if music was my solace, it became my work again as well. We had debt from the remodeling and cancer treatments, and I needed to get full time work fast. Within two weeks of Gordon's death, a friend called to say that a local church was looking for an organist; I should apply. I knew nothing about the organ, but the touch is similar to the harpsichord and I was too tired to be afraid of what I did not know. I called. An extremely personable fellow didn't seem at all taken aback when I said that I did not know how to play the organ, and suggested that even with this initial shortcoming, it might be manageable. I didn't have the courage to tell him that due to faulty wiring (gift of M.S.), my six foot span from head to toe left knees and feet like a colonial settlement—remote and surprisingly independent. I showed up for a choir rehearsal, sight-read through an evening's worth of music which was ridiculously simple compared to the opera scores I was used to reading, and got the job.

One day, after I had been working for the church for several months trying to befriend my feet so I could manage the pedals, I walked into the sanctuary to practice and suddenly saw it for the first time. *I knew this place.* I had dreamt this exact setting 20 years before, during the initial episode of M.S. The dream had detailed the layout of the chancel and narthex and the precise positions of the organ and piano. (The ebony grand in the dream would be a piano I purchased years later, eventually moving with it to Southern Oregon, loaning it to this church. Did I, the dreamer, know that?) Even the distinctive bright green carpet and the number and design of the stair steps to the altar were a match. I had been here before. Only in the dream, the purpose of the scene had been to serve as a setting for an elaborate sacred processional glorifying the crucifixion. This had seemed a particularly quixotic, if not downright heretical choice of dream imagery for a Jew, so it was a dream I worked with and remember well.

At the time, I understood the image to be speaking to a kind of priestly initiation one goes through when entering into a deeper relationship with disease. When one is willing, and extremely fortunate, illness can reveal itself as an element of divine syntax, enfolding both one's tissue and awareness in a new and humbling grammar of being. I had understood the dream to be addressing the matter of healing both my failing hands and spirit, that the scenario's subject was my own mortality and resurrection into a larger sense of myself, whether I lived or died.

I didn't know, and of course could not have known, that this same scene would be the one I would casually step into on a spring afternoon 20 years later as a widow. The crucifixion and early death had been Gordon's, not mine. Except that it was mine as well, which is what this writing is all about, for here I was, in this curiously overlapped church, working at a brand new job, trying to resurrect a broken heart. In this first reentry into the collective world of work and performance after Gordon's death, I was not only sitting at my own piano in the sanctuary, I was being paid to discover the huge and transporting sounds of a church organ—a bald appeal to the divine through music.... Of course.

This capricious unweaving of the concrete world continued to play itself out in manifold ways during the first several years of widowhood. Discrete realities became suddenly slippery, intersecting at odd angles, assuming unpredictable dimensions. Formerly disconnected events now resonated in a common web of deeply felt purpose. Nothing was an isolated experience anymore. It felt like some invisible force was knitting all possibilities into being, a woven substructure that lay out of sight and nearly out of mind. Memories, time, space, all loosened so that I was often not quite sure what or where I was. Given this warping whimsy of my world since Gordon's death, to awaken and find myself in a dream 20 years old made a certain uncanny sense. Shit, why not? We who have suffered a deep loss walk between worlds.

I began to talk to myself, quite a lot. Coaching. "I can do it" became and remains a constant refrain. As soon as I hear myself say it, I know it's getting air time because there is a real question whether I can or not. I became the Howard Cosell of my own life, reporting to the empty air around me how I was doing. This new verbal obbligato probably popped up as a substitute for a shared sense of my "isness." For 17 years, I had heard back from Gordon not only how I was, but that I was. I needed to hear some voice in the silence of the day, even if it was only my own. And I needed that voice to believe in me.

On the church choir director's recommendation, I took Galen to audition for a man who had just written a musical and was having a hard time finding boys who could sing and act. Galen was interested, so I called about it. I explained that Galen's dad had just died and that any test he faced right now, including an audition for a stranger, needed to be offered with respect for how incomprehensibly vulnerable he was. There was no way of knowing how a stage experience would prove out—it might or might not be good medicine. After a brief pause, the man on the other end of the phone said, "I understand exactly. My wife died two months ago." And so, Michael and I met. Through the most alarmingly tenuous moments of our madness, we held one another's safety by phone. We would call one another for "sound checks." To know that we each still were, that the particular shape of this day's weirdness was recognizable to someone else, and that neither was cruising off some edge where no one could fish us back again. It is in this sense that we loved each other through the worst of it—by simply being there. Answering the phone and being; holding the fragments of our lives in Ma Bell's lines.

The church choir director was also the director of a large community choir that was looking for a second pianist for the duo piano version of *Carmina Burana*. I got the job. It is a huge and largely percussive piano score, and was perfect medicine for the relentlessly intense assignment of simply getting through a day. I could lean deep into the keys, fly through the octaves and feel such joyous relief in the oversized, outlandish enormity of the sound. The piece was almost big enough to capture me, to throw a lasso around the pain of this horrible hole inside and pull it out—a musical exorcism of emptiness.

We played to full houses in widely publicized performances and the fragility of widowhood temporarily fell away in the boisterous, bawdy triumph of the music itself. I felt neither self-conscious nor fearful; my energy was drawn down, way too lean and focused for any gratuitous anxiety. I just felt the utter relief of feeling sewn into the sounds of the voices and instruments around me. The opportunity was heaven-sent. Music was gathering me in, pointing the way home. I have made a living (haphazard though it has been) as a full time performing professional ever since. And with Galen's unexpected opportunity to sing and act in Michael's musical (a story about a lonely young boy grieving his absent father) he, too, was the beneficiary of the mysterious ability of music to heal—the ineffably sublime world of sound calling hearts home. The stage as sanctuary set Galen on the path of a professional child actor.

When I wasn't practicing, I was staring out the front window—just staring. A determination to make a move in any particular direction was too difficult a decision. So I stood, unable to line up energy or direction, for hours. I watched the grass on the lawn, the trees growing up from it, the shift of clouds and light over it all, sometimes noticing the birds that flew by.

Although the birds had been merely peripheral ornaments to the passing scene, one morning they slipped into much sharper focus. They seemed to want my attention, to be trying to tell me something. An iridescent green hummingbird, completely out of his season, began to appear at the window in the living room where I practice. When I first noticed him, I had been completely absorbed in working over a piece at the piano, my back to the windows. Suddenly, the back of my neck began to tingle: hair raised, shoulders awake. When I looked up to see what in the heck was throwing me into high alert, the hummingbird was there, looking in at me. For days, the hair on my neck would tell me if he had made an appearance, and when I turned to look, he would be there. I knew it was Gordon. And there we were, with the damned pane of glass between us, and time and space between us, and no way to reach one another but through this voiceless, winged symbol. I felt grateful and utterly heart-broken.

A brilliantly colored male ring-necked pheasant began visiting the tangled brush beyond the lawn. Strutting, patrolling his space, watchful. Gordon. Spectacular birds, drawn in close, making loud and uncustomary visitations, speaking in a stranger language than I could answer, about a love I couldn't see. I felt their unsettling, reassuring purpose—somewhere, he still was. I became a regular at the farmer's grange, laying in bird feeders and seed, eager to beckon these messengers from worlds I could not enter, petitioning his nearness.

This feeling about Gordonness in the birds' visitations was not without precedent. Just before Gordon had left in September for that last fateful trip to Portland, we had been talking about healing and hope in the living room, me exhorting Gordon not to give up, when a large male quail suddenly smacked into the glass doors behind us. He broke his neck. This never occurs. To the smaller finches and chickadees, yes, but never to quails. My heart sank, and I could barely look at Gordon. He said very quietly, "Jen, sometimes these things just happen, and we can't control them. Nor do we get to know why." We both knew we were flying into windows. Now I notice birds.

Driving back home late after the first performance of the *Carmina Burana*, this abiding intuition of bird signifiers for Gordon surrendered to a deeper ratification. On one of the last stretches of country road, just before reaching home, I felt Gordon inside me. Loving, reassuring... *there*. And I thought, oh my God, this is more intimate than sex. You are in me, loving deeper than clumsy flesh can go, with me in the very fiber of my being. Clutching the steering wheel in grateful amazement, I was showered in a blessed moment of grace. And it was all I got. I have haunted that stretch of road ever since with a hungry heart, hoping that when I'm coming home again *this* time, maybe just this next gift of a time, he might meet me there. My heart's deepest desire is etched on an unknowing stretch of asphalt. Why do we do things like that? Now that this is voiced, it seems like a fragile and foolish hope. But it is all I've had, so I have clutched it tight to my heart. I want to be found again. . . . Oh God, I still do.

When I wasn't standing and staring, or practicing, or forgetting what I was supposed to be doing next, I was running. I had been a runner for the whole of our marriage, schlepping my running shoes on every overseas junket. I have been a regular hoofer at extreme altitude in the Peruvian Andes and among the lions on the Maasai Mara. Neither terribly smart, but both necessary, it seemed. The running had stopped during the last months of Gordon's illness, but started again with a vengeance after his death. I couldn't put enough miles under my feet; I ran daily until I was exhausted. Our home is surrounded by miles of orchards, some planted by my ancestors, and as I ran, I screamed to the trees. I knew these trees, this earth, and I trusted this spaciousness to bear my outrage full volume—they were my history and they could give me this. And so I ran, and yelled and wept, and committed a violent act of remaining alive. Wearing myself out became the biggest daily test of whether I really was anymore or not. The earthy expanse of the orchards wrapped sufficient enormity around my terror and my fury, allowing the violated paths of my heart to play themselves out in a daily exorcism of God's Big Mistake.

> *Whoever in the hell You are, why the fuck did You take him?*
>
> *Why, damn it, why?*
>
> *Gordon, why did you leave me?*
>
> *Oh God, what did I do wrong?*
>
> *I told you that Galen and I would make it, but damn it, Gordon, I'm not sure.*
>
> *HOW are we going to do it?*
>
> *I am sorry, oh God, Gordon, so sorry for every piece of loving you that I failed.*
>
> *Gordon, I'm sorry. Please forgive me.*
>
> *I'm so sorry.*

Often as I ran, a ring-necked pheasant would flush from the grasses at roadside, and I would feel Gordon answering my complaint. "Sometimes these things just happen." Shit. . . . a pheasant. So grateful for the sense of his nearness and so dreadfully sad at its form.

And then, every once in a while, the Unthinkable Thought: *Relief.* The idea that the release from bondage to illness, even to a loving partner, would come zinging in and I would feel a blissful sense of freedom. Alone! Rapturous! Everything ahead of me was all mine, no obligations to anyone else except my son. God, what freedom! I could step into an enticingly undetermined future, one that was neither wearied nor failed. I had been given the great gift of getting to start over, brand new. And on those rare days of unbridled hope, I ran with the wild dispute of misery and guilty joy clanging in my traitorous heart.

Along with the why of Gordon's departure, there was also the where of it. Eventually the inert kitchen-window staring shaped itself into a concerted search. I knew if I opened my senses in some just-right way, I could find him. He was there in existence, somewhere. I just needed to find that where. I stared at the edges of form, watching for essence, looking just beyond the finest fibrils of brush, just beyond the leaf-tips of trees, past the density of air, the organic and visible world—somewhere, just out of sight. He must be there. And so I called out to him with my heart, and stood, watching. Calling, reaching, watching—for minutes, hours, days. . . . years.

> *Gordon, do you hear me?*
>
> *Do you FEEL me?*
>
> *ARE YOU OK? Oh God, please let this passage be full and right and blessed beyond measure for this wonderful being. Protect him. Guide him. Bring him blessed and safe to where he needs to be.*

Gordon, I'm here and I will always love you.

Always.

Oh Lord, if my prayer in any way hinders his path to his next right manifestation, please forgive me. Please God, let everything be wholly right and well for him. In its perfect and painless rightness. Please.

Gordon, I'm trying. I don't want to hold you where you can't be, but God, how I miss you.

One day, when I was absorbed in this effort to pierce the veil, a female quail stepped in front of the feeder to eat, and immediately rolled down the rocky incline. She worked her way back up to the feeding station, lost balance, rolled downhill once more. She was missing a leg. As I stood looking for Gordon, I knew she was me. Dusty from her failure, she tried again and again to do what she could not. In her blind determination to survive, begging a balance she would never have again, she was unable to do more than stumble and starve. I will never forget her.

Looking Back VI
June, 2011

__Michael:__ Birth and death are partners in nature. We accept them in that context. I, personally, find it difficult to see death as a constant companion to my life. Maybe because of the way we so readily accept life as good and death as bad in our culture, we don't allow death its rightful seat among us. In nature, though, it works. It works fine and I think we'd just as soon keep it that way.

It would make sense that with Gordon's death, you'd look for him in nature. Whatever flimsy purchase you had on your life as mother, widow and wage-earner was grounded in these sweet reminders of the naturalness of death. The suspicion that Gordon was never far away. Feeling his consciousness and embrace in the unwavering stare of the hummingbird as you played piano. Sensing his gesture in the bend of a leaf. He was making his presence known to you in all that surrounded you on your rural property.

Maya's presence was announced with flaring energy up my spine and neck, in the same way that you felt the unequivocal tingly neck presence of Gordon's visitations on the other side of the window from the hummingbird. Interesting, too, that the bird songs and animal entreaties that were once in the aural background of your daily marriage were now front and center. Your sensitivity to every aspect of the natural environment around you was quite phenomenal. Always alert to Gordon's appearance in the abiding presence of every bird, every animal. Animals know, don't they?!

I think we each looked to the eternal for healing. We shared the same two touchstones in our journeys through darkness, nature and music, knowing that their beauty persists long after our tenuous passage here on earth. I'm reminded of having read about how every note of music is contained within the sound of crashing waves and within the sound of the wind thanks to the way harmonics bounce off one another to create 'the sound of all.' You looked to the eternal to heal your aching heart, knowing that your body's wisdom couldn't fail you. You were in a state beyond mere suggestibility. Living side by side with death opened you to all of nature. Nature lives with death and we try our absolute best not to.

And don't our partners still speak to us in all of nature's suggestions? In everything that is eternal? "More intimate than sex." We are surrounded by this weave of *belonging to a family beyond that which is experienced by the senses. Nature and music keep pointing us in this direction.*

But I know that the messengers in nature and music's grand understanding still remained airy and unearthly substitutes for the physical nearness of what our cells were screaming for. Just please touch me again to let me know you're there.

CHAPTER 6

All This Love and Nowhere to Put It

How can so many things possibly break? Sound checks. How can six months last so interminably long? WHEN will this get better?

There is a hole that gets torn into you when your beloved dies. Bones grieve, marrow mourns, and tissue hangs off, flayed and raw, unable to intend more than surviving. The day after his dad's death, Galen drew death itself. He knew what she looked like, and he wanted me to see. She was implacable, serene, unthreatening. Galen knew. Whatever had claimed his dad had an integrity beyond our questioning.

But as the days passed, initial inscrutability felt more and more like a theft. We were facing down a plate of cardboard instant pasta one night when he buttonholed the real problem with our circumstance. "I have all this love, Mom, and nowhere to put it." That was it. It was less being loved, than being able to love.

There is a horrible ache to empty expression; always searching, reaching out to the vanished beloved. Our hearts were haunted. We had been privileged to live in a matrix of enormous love, exchanging depth and joy and suffering with the unthinking ease of each breath. Now, the field had suddenly contracted and everything about us felt squeezed and small. We were squeezed and small. The center of our lives had disappeared. At first we choked, overfull with this unexpressed love, and then we became hollow. It is a terrible progression.

The phone answering machine had Gordon's voice on it, and I kept it there for the sound of him, to have him in the field, somewhere. It was the voice of the one who had loved us, and who had held our hearts safe. It was the only remnant of the life we'd led, the one that had been intact and whole. But this soon became unsettling for family calling to check in, so I surrendered the sound, and then there was nothing but the vast and empty silence.

In that silence, the world of phone machines, cars, clocks, hot water heaters, vacuum cleaners, ovens, washing machines, computers began to break. The whole energetic field in our house had changed with Gordon's death and all the damned machines marked it. If it plugged in or had a motor, it broke. It was a bizarre kind of mechanical chaos and it made sense. Even the family labrador, loyal and impossibly wise companion through the whole of our marriage, died. Everything had to be repaired or replaced, and in the process of tending to it all, the world became more fully mine. I had to become capable of managing all these things, alone. It was a nerve-wracking initiation into the world of single parenting, of learning to face and deal with breaking and fixing. I hated it.

In the midst of our unraveling home, as I was trying to figure out which organizations really needed death certificates from me as I sought to disconnect Gordon from the world, I was also finishing a lawsuit that he had undertaken on our behalf as he was dying. It was damnable business. It made me tired, angry, confused and very sad.

One of the physicians hired as a witness by Gordon's attorneys had grossly overcharged for his services. What should have been a $300 bill for services came in at $32,000, subtracting a huge sum from the small settlement that Gordon had fought for on Galen's and my behalf. Gordon's lawyers were appalled, embarrassed, and without recourse.

I wrote the doctor. I told him about us, about how this suit had resulted from a misdiagnosis by a friend. Our two families had shared wonderful events together, and now this terrible, irretrievable error. I told him that the suit had not been undertaken without our friend's unhesitating agreement; Gordon had no choice but to travel this path. How single-parenting as a freelance musician, Galen and I would need financial help to survive. That in his grief, our friend had left the profession. I wanted this man to realize what enormous pain, in all directions, had surrounded Gordon's even deciding to pursue legal action. I got no reply.

And gradually, in the course of trying to figure out how to do all these tasks, of chopping through the thicket tying Gordon to the world, I lost focus and couldn't think. I was too damned tired and got progressively more woolly-headed. I began to wonder what had happened to my memory, because it was not anywhere within reach. There seemed no graceful option but surrender to this appalling new stupidity. I had only enough grey matter to hang onto commitments for work and the tasks of mothering immediately in front of me.

I would start the day with a list of things to be done, and find my energy had vanished well before even a few had been accomplished. I would drive by storefronts, knowing the errand that I needed to do there, and just pass on by. The effort of opening the car door and getting out, let alone squaring up to the task that awaited, no matter how simple, was more than I could manage. Essence was hemorrhaging.

After several months of this, I began to worry about my head. I reentered graduate school to see if Gordon's death had indeed transformed me into a mental marshmallow. Reed College, where I had been enrolled in a demanding masters program before our move, is a six-hour drive from Southern Oregon. Within the first two weeks of summer school, I had trimmed it to four. Galen spent weekdays with friends' families and I came home on weekends. It was rugged for us both, fraying the edges of a sadly tentative bond between us. I had been too depressed to be very present emotionally after his dad died, and now I was physically absent as well. But the schooling seemed an imperative: I had to do it. I wanted to refasten my untethered mind, I wanted to finish what I had begun, and I wanted to own the hope of greater financial ease for Galen and me with this graduate degree. There was a warrior who was struggling to survive, and this was a battle I knew she must win. I needed to believe in her, so I just saddled up the Subaru and drove, fast, and a lot. It was part of my debt to the gift of having been Gordon's partner. I wanted to be honorable and heroic, for all three of us.

But before this fairly frantic extroversion in search of my mind and our future began, Galen and I were given an extraordinary reprieve. After days, weeks, forever, of our shuffling on the seabed with no air supply, one of my very dearest friends marched in with a GOOD IDEA. Betsy had booked a casita for all of us in Akumal, Mexico. In spite of my worried protests that I couldn't leave jobs that were still so new to me, she insisted. Her children were Galen's best buddies from birth, she knew what Galen and I needed and she was not taking no for an answer. She's Texan. We went. She scooped us out of our bewilderment and put her children and Galen and me on a plane with her, bound for Mexico.

It wasn't a good idea. It was a SPECTACULAR IDEA. It was the smartest damned gift anyone could have given us, and certainly one of the kindest. It had been impossible to conceive of an escape from grief—it has no back door. But here we were in the remarkable beauty of a remote seaside village, with its soft beaches and bays full of flamboyant tropical fish, with no assignment but to soak it all in. Grief was tricked. Betsy's gift had thrown us a line, and for one wonderful week, two lost divers found their way to the surface. We could breathe.

Travel is miraculous balm for a wounded heart. Nothing in sight reminded us of home and so we were free of it. We laughed, ate, and swam, and by week's end had been poured back into ourselves. For all the anguish and confusion after Gordon's death, this unexpected adventure was definitely the golden counterweight. For a brief and blessed time, our world had found a right and glorious gravity again.

CHAPTER 7

Chop Wood, Carry Water

Busting Rock, Planting Trees—Telephone Poles and Garbage Trucks—Staying Alive—Bald

Several times during that first year and even through the second, family and friends drove from Portland, Sebastopol, and L.A. to help fix up our lives. My sisters-in-law and Betsy came to help cook, clean, prune roses, and apologize to my thoroughly neglected yard, sort bills and organize our seemingly endless chaos, love up Galen and give me rest. They also joined brothers and a brother-in-law to finish a bathroom, install the woodstove, tile the kitchen, and help my father pile and burn the huge amount of construction debris left behind.

I could not have done any of this. In spite of my parents' earnest desire to help in any way they could, including watching Galen while I had evening rehearsals (often), our lives were tangled in fraying edges that littered the field, dirtying up hope. Things to be done jumbled up in every direction. It was impossible not to trip over all that was unfinished. I had gotten in the habit of stumbling, it was all I knew how to do; fall, bruise but not break, sidle around the edges of the chaos, and then get up and go again. Figuring out what to do with the remains of Gordon's work and life (boxes and boxes and boxes) or the still-to-be-emptied-then-sold house in Portland, or the unpacked boxes of my music and cookware (where were they in this mess?), and bedding and furniture and, and, and—it was totally overwhelming. These were just the routine sorting and solving tasks of widowhood (I guess), but the psychic weight they laid on top of parenting, working, not losing the important bills, keeping track of a four-acre rural spread with a failing well and broken irrigation lines was damned near crippling. It was tonnage I did not have the strength to budge.

None of the work my family did for us could have been done without their help, because I didn't have the strength to figure out who to ask for assistance, let alone the means to pay for it. I was managing to keep the electric bills and mortgage paid, get myself to work and school, Galen to play rehearsals, and feed us both. This was as long a list as I could carry. I don't know how people in this kind of situation do it without the blessing of help that just comes. It has to, or the fatigue can become crushing and plummet straight into despair. And even with help and lots of love, despair hangs close, watching, intimating the inconceivable option.

Many times as I was driving, I had the vague sense that there were a number of telephone poles along my route that might have my name on them. They could, couldn't they? I didn't actively engage ideas of suicide, but I did actively lobby some part of me against it. I reminded myself that I did not admire this apparent cheat of a choice, that I would never be able to rectify such an error karmically, and that of course I wasn't even thinking these thoughts. I was all Galen had. And then I would successfully pass another telephone pole, relieved. I can't believe I'm writing this. But it was there, and I had to armor against a kind of sleazy seduction to just quit. God, I was tired.

Galen, too, flirted with edges that were terrifying to me. We had been in the constant care of a healer who practices classical medicine, a system of diagnosis and treatment akin to acupuncture, mapped by the pulses of energy meridians. I credit him with helping keep us both alive. He worked with us shamanically as well, agreeing that mustering the will to want to stay was as much at issue as the physical ability to do so.

Sometime in this first year, Galen came down with a cold that turned into pneumonia. We had been monitoring it, and then suddenly, I knew he was losing the battle. He had fallen asleep on my bed where I could keep an eye on him before carrying him off to his own bed, when I felt a shift in the room. He was standing at the threshold, deciding whether to live or die. When someone is making this decision, a very distinctive smell enters the atmosphere. Such sensory hyper-awareness is like a rattlesnake's rattle. You don't ever have to have heard it before to know what it is, or what it means. I knew this smell because it had been there when Gordon had decided to die. I was absolutely terrified.

I called Yeshosha. He drove over immediately, sat on the bed with my sleeping child, and interceded on behalf of life. He told me that of course he couldn't make this decision for Galen, but that he would argue its advantages to the best of his abilities.

Then he entered a trance to make the case. After an eternity, he returned to my world and said he thought Galen would stay. And with that, he left. The next morning, Galen perked up and set about being a child again. I aged a thousand years.

Later that year, when Galen was visiting his cousins in Portland, he joined them on their morning walk to school. This involves crossing a very heavily-trafficked thoroughfare in a crosswalk that did not have a light. Morning rush-hour traffic had stopped in both directions for my family entourage to make their way across and Galen skipped on ahead, eager to beat the girls to the other side. A garbage truck, ignoring the stopped traffic, pulled around it all, passed on the right, and barreled toward Galen. My sister-in-law said she screamed, looked up, and saw Gordon reach toward Galen to pull him to the side as the truck flew by. When they got to school, the phone board was lit up with callers wanting to know if the little boy had survived.

One fellow called my sister-in-law later in the day to ask how she was doing. Witnessing this had rattled him so, he had barely been able to work. Galen said he hardly felt the truck brush him; it didn't seem so bad. He just kind of hopped out of the way. Others count it a miracle.

Edges. Playing edges—close about for both of us, but neither of us choosing or getting to go over. Wanting to stay has been damned hard work. For both of us.

Maybe because we both now really know that living is a choice, and because we know about loss, we are impatient with the tendency to masquerade petty discontents as issues that truly matter. They don't. Neither of us is any good at chitchat. We can't do it, and people feel this.

In the beginning, we became pariahs, walking deep with the ugly truth that no one wants to know: we all die. Our depression scared many away. That was fine, because if they did not have the strength to simply be still and abide with us, they didn't need to be in our world. But thankfully, a blessed, compassionate few stayed the course with us, unafraid of having nothing to say. They simply reached out, not presuming to claim any ultimate wisdom about the rightness or wrongness of Gordon's death or any other death, or death as an idea at all. They just loved us up, patiently and with boundless kindness. These were people who knew what we now knew as well, people who had lost beloveds they hadn't been able to imagine living without. We become a collection, those of us who have suffered this knowing. We can feel it from one another, and the quality is this: there is no judgement and no pretension to certainty. None. And there is a willing drive toward the outrageous. We are a very short leap away from edges that have to be funny in order to survive them. We are the people of fearless humor, and it is this that has kept us alive.

One of the most aggressive acts of biting back into life that overcame me in the first months was the rush to stick roots in the earth, big ones. Trees, lots and lots of trees. Galen used to ride in terror with me, afraid that any nursery would be the occasion of yet another planting detour from the supposed agenda of the moment. "Oh Mom, come on, not another one!" It became his lament through the spring, because I couldn't stop myself.

We live on four acres of mean earth. It is rocky, clay soil, unfriendly to much of anything other than poison oak and oaks themselves, and the deliberate attempts local farmers have made at orchards. I wanted leaves that would rustle and sing in the breeze; I wanted color, I wanted variety, I wanted hope. Aspens, redbuds, cedars, pines, maples, a pomegranate, smoke tree and countless bushes; I bought 'em all and stuck 'em in.

Dad had a long iron digging bar for busting rock, and I just hammered away at the damned earth until it would give enough to stick some hapless living thing in it. I apologized to them all, telling them that this was it; I wasn't going to do more than cover them up, because I couldn't. They'd have to figure out the food and watering themselves. I told them to be tough and survive, that I believed in them, and that they needed to be gritty and just do it. It was incredible therapy, from the enormous effort of hoisting the iron bar, let alone wielding the damned thing effectively, to laying in the toughened hope that some of these trees would actually survive. Some have, so far. I love them for it.

Lots of Galen firsts were happening: his first performance of Michael's musical, his first Y basketball game, his first belly-bouncing on an inner tube behind the boat at the lake, his first band concert on his new saxophone. Lots of them, and each one tore a piece out of me as I watched this beautiful child, so capable and courageous, this wonderful boy who would have been the pride and joy of his doting father. They were both cheated.

Gordon had been an NCAA scholar-athlete in basketball, one of 12 in the nation. He had been a swim coach in high school at one of the most prestigious swim clubs in Pasadena. The physical world belonged to him, and it would have belonged to Galen, too, had his father been here. As it was, I managed one season of Y-basketball and then flat-lined on any more lessons or practices for anything. I mustered energy to get him to his play rehearsals, but that was it. I just couldn't do more. An inheritance that should have invited in the physical world with joy and genuine competence hasn't opened to him. Galen deserved his dad cheering him on, shooting hoops with him, swimming with him, listening to him practice—loving him. I have felt this terrible theft every time I am an audience to Galen doing something new. As he's moaned thousands of times, "It's not fair, Mom. It's just not fair." Nope. Finding fair has been pretty damned difficult for him. I guess it's been undercover these past six years.

We inhabited a world marked by absence. For all that I was aggressive about chasing down graduate school to try and reel in my mind, my physical well-being was suffering cheats of its own. Galen had lost ready access to the delight and discipline of becoming a young athlete, and I had lost physical intimacy. Both our bodies mapped loss. Each of us was starved for touch. I hugged him what I thought was a lot, but it was not as much as two parents hugging, and wasn't anywhere near the rough and tumble wrestling of father and son. And truth be told, I didn't have much to give because my easy rapport with my own body had withered as well. My skin became excruciatingly sensitive to touch. Any simple pat on the back became a gift, measured beyond anything I am sure the giver could have imagined. There is a kind a body-breath that happens only in touch, and I was suffocating. This isn't sex I'm talking about here; it is the far more commonplace and perhaps far more essential need for easy and affectionate contact, pure and simple.

I watched the easy, unthinking bond of couples as they strolled down the sidewalk, through the shops in town, and felt like I was walking in a different world. I was stranded on an ice-flow at the other end of the earth, knowing how precious their casual claim on each other really was, knowing that they had no idea how lucky they were. I looked at families intact and I wanted to weep. Did they even have a clue how fortunate they were to have these moments together? Did they have any inkling that someday they would not? That it would end? Of course not. I became desperate for them not to waste this gift of time, all these people I didn't know, walking by.

For some reason, at a particular point in this whole process, my hair seemed a downright lie to the barrenness that had sucked the breath out of our days. About eight months in, I showed up for my scheduled haircut determined to have Laurie shave it all off. This choice had the same rash determination about it as needing to throw an iron bar at the earth and plant trees. I'd had it with this ridiculously superfluous curly mane on top of my head. It wasn't true and I wanted to get rid of it. She was horrified.

During the several occasions Galen and I had been in to see her, she had gotten to know and care about us, and as far as she was concerned, this was a really wrong turn. She wouldn't do it. I think she was afraid I would be terribly sorry once it was done, and that she couldn't participate in any more regret for me. Maybe she was right. But I knew what I wanted, lobbied ardently and unsuccessfully for it, and left with acceptably (to whom?) shorter hair, but nothing shocking. Once the moment had passed, it was over. I couldn't muster the urgency to put this forward again, and so I have remained thatched.

As I write this, I realize that part of the drive for shaving my head might have been fueled by the universally human urge to bear the truth of inexpressible pain in one's body. Certainly there is a psychic truth to the notion of tearing one's hair— overwhelming circumstances drive strange choices—but I also had the Maasai women I'd lived with close at heart. They are tall and lean, like me, beautiful, STRONG, and bald. These women have seen it all, suffered it all, and they survive, fearless. I thought of them often during this passage into widowhood, and may well have been reaching to pull their unflinching walk with the world into mine, to own the same ferocious capacity to see it all and survive, upright, wide awake, unbroken.

> *What more? What more was there in this first year? I don't remember. We made it. Maybe that's all that counts.*

Looking Back VII
2011

Michael: *What was it about simple touch that you needed and appreciated so much? Was that contact like a bridge between two continents over a tempestuous ocean? Were you most moved by the physical sensation of the touch itself, or the tenderness of the gesture?*

Jennifer: *Wow. Touch as a bridge. Maybe. Did I feel like an island? Absolutely—except for you. Because you were as fully whacked as I, our contact was my lifeline. Was I moved by touch itself, or the kindness implied in the gesture? Some of both, but mostly it was a matter of skin on skin. I had been in an intimate and loving marriage for 17 years. To have that ready contact removed all of a sudden was wrenching. It took months, maybe the first couple of years, for my skin to toughen up into the absence of touch. Initially, the nerve receptors were wild for contact; simple, kindly reassurance of our commonness. We're not a terribly touchy culture, so that ache was a constant. My skin became foreign and unfriendly terrain, never at ease or comfortable. Neither was the woman within it. Nothing about me or my life felt right. Period.*

CHAPTER 8

Ashes, Moving On

In the midst of fall that first year, as the season changed and leaves withered and took to the winds, I could feel a surrender happening for me as well. I began to think about scattering Gordon's ashes. The ugly brown plastic box that had been roosting in various uncomfortable places in our home was now perched on the kitchen windowsill, stupidly eloquent in its awkward claim on our attention.

We had an uneasy relationship to one another, the box and I, not unlike the distressing substitute of the cremation casket for my husband. I couldn't make sense of this lifeless plastic thing that contained the remains of my husband. I knew it was important, but I did not know what to do with that importance. After awhile, I didn't know what that importance really was anymore. The damned box just felt confining and untrue. It made me confused and terribly sad and out of step with myself. I wanted Gordon (if it mattered) and Galen and me to be able to move on in the most blessed of ways to whatever next was ours to do. Gordon was and was not there. I wasn't sure where Gordon was, but if any part of ashes in plastic interfered with his freedom to move full and free into a greater somewhere, I wanted to give him that. The box made less and less sense. Whatever of him it might still be keeping close no longer belonged in plastic. The whole stand-in of ashes for the man was absurd, wasn't it?. . . except that I wasn't sure the elision wasn't real or I would not have had to wear myself down into this surrender. If there was a whisper of isness or brushes of his texture in these ashes, they belonged in the world—given to air, given to earth, knit into the organic movement of life.

By mid-winter, it was time. An internal clock had ticked off the end of a willing agreement to sustain the confusion about something I just could not comprehend. The question had lost its mana to confound anymore. Galen didn't evince any feeling for the box mattering, so it seemed time to clear this out-of-joint prop from the stagecraft of our lives. The scene was changing, and the box and its contents needed to pass on as well.

Besides being consonant with the seasonal rhythm, being able to do this was surely in part the outcome of an outright assignment to move on. Yehosha had been a constant advocate for forward movement, encouraging us to release our history with Gordon, to LET IT GO (a voice akin to Betsy's in its self-assured certainty) that we might be able to step more fully into present time rather than straddling borders between worlds. As impossible as this request was (and one I felt to be downright naive, given the enormity of comprehending this loss), I believe now that he was arguing for our lives, knowing how precarious our purchase truly was.

Mid-week, some mid-January day (I think it was January, about a year had passed), Galen had left for school, the morning sky was threatening and it seemed time. If I did it now, rain would water in the ashes and they would belong to the earth before Galen returned home in the afternoon. It seemed right. I got out the hammer and called the funeral home, asking how to open the box. It was not hard. Why did I think it would be? I had been working up to this for months. This wasn't like losing a body, like death; this was just opening a box. I didn't even need the hammer. Deceptively, disappointingly simple. I took the box apart and there it was—a plastic sack of ashes and bone bits, quick-tie at the top. Not even loose and alarming in the first moments of being revealed, but packaged in a baggy, a last icon of our culture—death as a commodity held at the emotional remove of a plastic bag.

I pulled it out and headed outdoors into the pregnant morning. Early on the day that Gordon began to die, I had asked him what kind of service he wanted and where he wanted his ashes spread. He had already traveled beyond the importance of my questions, and simply replied, hastily, "Under the oak tree. That would be fine." And so on a mid-week morning in the dark of winter, I headed to the oak to honor what I know mattered far more to me than to him.

But once I stepped outside, some agent of divine trickery began to pour sand in my legs. What the heck was I doing? Even though his ashes were presented in plastic, reaching in to scatter them breached this social fiction of antiseptic order, so that my hard-won certainty, the clear conviction of readiness to do this, fled as I actually began. As the morning air grew dense with approaching rain, I began to circle the tree. Wandering in an unthinking spiral, feeling suddenly heavy and confused, I stepped into a disquieting realization. I was in deeper than I had imagined with this apparently straightforward matter. I didn't know what this business of ashes really meant. As somebody's elephantine feet (surely not mine) paced the scrabbled earth around the tree, the thief of my morning resolve gradually stepped from the shadow: in holding Gordon's ashes in my hand, all of me got caught. There was no choice but to wrestle with ciphering the importance of this act, and I was once again face to face with the enormous effort of letting go. God, how many times would I be here, LETTING GO, again and again and again?? Touching the tail of death's garment had thrown me back into the impossibly vast landscape of loss. Like all the days that had led up to this one, although I had laid an unsteady track, I needed to simply move on and finish the task. Keep going. That was the deal I'd made with God. It was about to rain.

Besides the sabotage of yet another reckoning, I was unnerved by wavering discernment. A piece of my heart shadowed my steps, wondering over my left shoulder whether I needed a witness to this ceremony in order to imbue it with sacred meaning. Would the Divine feel cheated at being short-changed of an audience? Would Gordon? Was there a Right Way here?... Something I should have known but did not? It felt strangely empty, doing this alone. And perhaps, that was some of the confusion. Fear of righteous insufficiency masked exquisite loneliness. God was fine. *I* was the one who needed the ballast of someone near, holding the ground of this moment and my part in it as I stepped into the surreal world of scattering my husband's ashes. Unsure how I was supposed to do this, I said prayers as I walked, gave thanks, asked forgiveness, and spread ashes and bone. Although gray and damp, the gestures felt akin to offering pollen or cornmeal to the morning sun. Gratitude and surrender, both.

I knew this was holy business, I just didn't know which side of the sacred I was inscribing. Was I addressing it as sunrise or sunset? His life or mine? Which part of good-bye was this? And which part of God was I talking to as I did it? The Creator? The Transformer? The Destroyer? Or the gray air between them all that enveloped me and the tree and these ashes? The rain began to fall.

I was wearing jeans and a flannel shirt, and old running shoes. In the onset of wind and rain, ashes began sticking to my shoes, washing over my clothes. I watched myself beginning to wear the odd gray essence of what had been my beloved. The confusion became exponential. Was some of his spirit still here, filtered fine in this last outline of who he had been? Or was this God's joke, shoving me in the face with the absurdity of such deeply grooved grief? Was I getting lost in the complexity of something that did not want to be layered in sorrow anymore?

I covered my track with dried rose petals, ending with the last and largest gift of ash under a white rock I'd set next to the oak tree. The rock had been just outside the bedroom window where Gordon died; surely it carried his trace. I wanted it to mark the last piece of him. Then I came back inside, tattooed with ash, not at all sure what I had just done. I didn't tell Galen.

As winter moved toward spring, the rabbi called one afternoon to ask whether Galen and I would care to do a marking ceremony. After one year has passed, members of the community who knew the deceased gather to leave stones at the gravesite. I had a sundial in the front yard, an iron sculpture of an Indian brave, arms uplifted, holding a musical staff with the bass notes of Gordon's favorite Telemann Sonata inscribed on it. It was the continuo line, the one I had played. The line missing was the solo recorder line, the one no longer in the air. The conductor's baton rested on the staff, marking shadows, seasons—absence. The Indian was "Mohican Boy," the protagonist, young hero, and wiseman of countless morning stories woven between Gordon and Galen. He was the heroic stand-in for a father telling his son about the world and how to live ethically, courageously, joyfully in it. Mohican Boy had been a very real presence in our lives as a family, and now he stood in our yard, the elegant and commanding gift of a talented metalworking friend who had created him from a note I had sent in the mail about Gordon's death. All the choices were his, and they were all achingly correct. This was Gordon's marker, and YES, we did want the ceremony.

We gathered on a cold Sunday after church services and schul at the synagogue, a ring of us in the blustery morning, standing in the grass around Mohican Boy. The rabbi talked about the importance of a year's passing, that coming to this moment had not only to do with surviving, but with remembering and moving on. He talked about the work Galen and I had done, achieving a hard won reprieve from the initial shocking days. Now we not only could afford to remember, but were obligated by love to do so. As the rabbi talked, I realized that even though we had made it through this first year, we had been scoured raw by it. In spite of his hopeful assertion that one year was a demarcation that invited us to move ahead now that the deep, organic grieving had been accomplished, I knew I had survived only by grace, and by a stoic, metallic kind of strength that bears a blind, unthinking commitment to ongoingness. I wanted the maturity I assumed he meant, but frankly, I was at a loss to understand what new expansiveness he was talking about. I knew, of course, that we were aiming for daylight—that the point was to resurrect into some greater delight in simply being—but I was mighty damned unclear about what that would feel like anymore.

Each of us had come with stones that meant something to us. After initial prayers, we used our stones to mark the relationship we had had with this wonderful man. We placed them in a pile, building a trail duck in his honor that we might remember, and that those who followed might know that this magnificent someone had walked this track in our lives. Each of us knit our hearts into the earth with this remembering. My yard has become hallowed because of it; it always was, of course, but now it is nuanced in this particularly exquisite way.

Once the stones were set, we left the cold and headed inside to throw Galen's dad a whopping party, because Galen said he would like that. We served up Gordon's favorite foods (Galen knew which), taped crepe paper and balloons to the ceilings and walls, turned up the music LOUD, and said YES to it all. Being alive. Having loved. Being here still. Galen was right.

Looking Back VIII
2011

Jennifer: *I am several more deaths in now, more experiences of ashes, and still, it is not a commonplace. The knowledge that the body is reduced to a small bag of particles doesn't remove the shock that this is the stand-in for the person you loved. I still don't know what to do with my uneasiness, so I choose to look the other way—to ignore the question. I am utterly at a loss to understand what ashes mean or where the beloved has gone. Holding the tension is more than I can bear, so I witness and move on.*

How did you reckon with Maya's ashes? Did it throw you as much as it did me? What do you do with it now? I guess what I'm really asking is, what in the heck do we make of death, Michael??

Michael: *I couldn't let go of the ashes for the longest time, so I separated it out: these ashes for the park where we first decided we were in love, these ashes for the backyard where we got married, these ashes for the ocean that we loved.*

In short, I couldn't let them all go in a singular whoosh of closure. Couldn't, and didn't. I knew that this ash and bone-chip pile was for me. Maya couldn't have cared less. It was for me to symbolically use to separate out our life paths. So, since they were for me, I drove around with them perched on the passenger seat. Most would view this as a perversity. I viewed it as a sedative. I viewed it as being as close as I could be to my remaining connection to her.

I would casually speak with her as if it were the most normal of things to do. Her silence was often my only answer. These gray-white ashes were the one tie to what was formerly us. I held on to them for at least a year, until the very last microscopic bit of ash was whipped up and out of its container and set free into the air to giggle in the wind currents as she most certainly would have done.

Throw me, though, it did. The ashes seemed such a sorry representation for the exquisite body, a paltry offering to substitute for the depth of the person. And a damnable exchange for the dreams we had of a life together.

But the ashes were all I had.

CHAPTER 9

Several Years After— Floods, Malaria, M.S., Getting By

One wonders why it is the aching moments that get remembered first. I know there were many light and goofy ones, ones where Galen and I were enfolded in the flow of a life that seemed good and kind. I know there were more and more of these moments. Why don't I remember them as well? Maybe because pain became a habit. It was the single way to keep what was left of him. All I had was this deep and sacred wound. If I let go of it, where was he? Where was I?

About two years in, I began to break. For all that I wanted to match the strength of the Maasai, I live with a different burden of consciousness, and am not one. Perhaps, sometimes, they break too. They must, mustn't they? In any case, I did. Somewhere between commuting to grad school and trying to manage the tangle of the rest of my life, I ended up in the back of an ambulance on a midnight junket to the local emergency room. One night, as I lay drifting off to sleep, I was overcome by alarming vertigo, unresponsive to increasingly frantic efforts to micro-adjust my errant head and torso into obedience. My world had gone into a tailspin and the thread that held me here was getting finer and finer. I managed to yell and awaken Galen, telling him to call 911 for help, and then I lay there, trying to will myself to hang onto a fast receding strength. I was floating away. The slightest movement produced overwhelming nausea. Galen watched as paramedics hoisted his thoroughly distressed mom from a bed she couldn't leave.

I was released after much medicine and less certainty one day later—possible repercussions of malaria, or dysentery—or despair. I think now that I'd just run over the edge; I had totally exhausted an ability to cope and I imploded. To have trespassed my limits so blindly was mighty sobering, but the truth was that I had lost touch with any sense of ease, anywhere in my life. In every direction I looked, it was all hard. In the service of a gallant living on, a heroic, making-the-best-of-a-tough-assignment, I had just flat outrun my strength and heart. In my driven determination to make things OK for us, I had made Galen's world suddenly far less secure. His dad was dead and his mom had gone out the door on a stretcher.

Eager to repair his confidence, I immediately stepped back into our familiar rhythm as soon as I returned home, reassuring him that I, by God, wasn't leaving him, and that this was a temporary anomaly. It was too terrifying to admit that I might be in deeper trouble than either of us wanted to face. For the time being, my bravado served as a convincing feint for us both.

But another few months down the line, more body tricks began to crop up, and I became afraid. I lost my sense of taste. No food, not even the most glamorous chocolate indulgence, tasted of anything but metal. It was terrifying. I saw my family physician and my dentist, both of whom were at a loss to explain or treat such a thoroughly singular symptom. I ate, of course, but very little; eating had become an eerie experience. The psychological truth of the symptom, however, was elegant. I had lost my taste for living. I was working hard at surviving, going forward with as much deliberate intelligence as I could muster, but it was all work. There was very little play in this schedule, and although the work I do is not without joy, there wasn't a baseline of well-being that sustained my efforts at a day. I had been running on empty for a very long time. Like the attack of vertigo, I wore through this; months later it righted itself, but none of us can say how. I knew that I was in trouble at the very organic core of myself but I just didn't know what to do about it. There was no one in my life to cover for the deep rest I needed.

And then it really unraveled and I was down for the count. Somewhere near the third year of widowhood, I was playing a beefy Bach postlude one Sunday morning when the notes began to disappear. I'd had trouble keeping the earlier hymns in place during this service, but had willed the notes to stay black and still. By the postlude, the music was no longer responsive to will. The notes ran off the page, out of sight. I caught edges of them, black wisps of what the page had held before it was erased by my failing vision. I stumbled to the finish, closed the music, and wept. The jig was up and I knew it. Nothing now was in its full outline: not the pews in the sanctuary, the friends in the choir watching and terribly concerned for me, not my hand gathering up my music to head home to figure out what to do next. Everything was becoming sieved in light and no contour was complete. Not one.

I began the standard battery of eye exams the next day, only to have the physician tell me that this was not a problem of the eye.

He sent me for an MRI. Something was wrong with my brain. He, of course, wouldn't hazard a guess about what that might be, so I left, pretty damned scared. The MRI showed lesions in both hemispheres of the brain, the scarring typical of M.S. Having feared that it might be another cancer in our lives, I was relieved. At least this was disease I knew from the inside. Even though I'd enjoyed nearly 20 years of remission, I had been initiated into the language of this illness, and I had once known how to listen. The God who spoke through my body and I had walked here before. I trusted that I could do this, no matter how far out my body went in this round of disintegration.

One of the seminars I had taken at Reed while commuting to finish graduate school was a study of madness in literature. Many of the characters in the texts we studied felt somehow familiar; I knew something about their madness and felt kindred with their despair. Concurrent with the literary task, we took up psychological analyses of these figures, applying current diagnostic categories to each character's situation. I suddenly realized why I had felt so at home with these testaments to distress. There I was, in D.M.S. Category IV, Post Traumatic Stress Disorder—a perfect fit, down to the last period in the description. Widowhood had felt like a besiegement, and I was weary unto a veritable madness. Every circuit I had, had been overrun and no agreement with an old and reliable order kept its contract anymore.

Having diagnosed myself in the classroom two summers before, facing the news of lesions in my brain now had a certain awful legitimacy about it. I didn't want this, had not meant to invite it, but couldn't act like I didn't understand where it might have come from.

I took a leave of absence from work (as if there was really any choice) and went home to try and heal. My meditation and my prayer became the passion to see all of Galen's face. Twenty years ago, when I had first been diagnosed with M.S., it had been the music in me, the Bach and Brahms that I heard and felt inside, that had pulled me forward into a fierce conviction to be well. That and the outrage that this unasked-for infirmity might infect the life of my new and beloved husband. This had not been part of the marriage contract and I couldn't let it happen to him; he deserved better from me. Now it was the certainty that I must see my son again. All of him. For both our sakes. Galen had the right to an alive and active mom, able to fully engage his emerging world. As with his dad 20 years before, this was non-negotiable. God owed me this.

Rather than receding into darkness, my field of vision was sieved into unbroken arrays of too-white light. All forms were broken into random bits, disconnected from any wholeness, any agreeable fiction of certainty. The metaphor was apt. The tangible field of "reality" is a fiction of sorts, an agreement we all make to see what we say is so and not believe anything else that we do not care to include in our assignments of normal. But it is all a negotiation—all of it, and I knew it. I knew it was a game we all played, had to play, except that as my visual field unraveled, so did my place in the game; I could not read the rules anymore. I couldn't read the world. All its outlines, the anchors that could help me put my feet down in the present moment, were fast disappearing. I could not get any forms to hold; all things were erasing themselves into a primeval state, some light-filled uroboric unity. I had gone too far away, lost and looking for Gordon, and now I needed to find my way back.

I changed my diet, began an intense practice of Tai Chi, meditated, underwent shamanic extractions and initiations, resumed regular bodywork, rested, and prayed. A lot. Members of the Methodist Church where I had played, and of the synagogue where Galen was studying for his bar mitzvah made us meals, cleaned our house, checked up on us. The minister even dropped by one afternoon to mow what had once been my lawn. Friends appeared in astoundingly generous ways and held us together. It was totally overwhelming. I had no idea there could be such willing gifts of time to help one another, and such generous love. I was on many prayer lists, and I felt it. It was palpable. The grace attending prayer is an astonishing experience of how profoundly connected we all are and how utterly stupid we are about it nearly all of the time. We are truly one another's keepers.

I held regular phone consultations with a psychic healer in San Diego who registered my physical state based on diet. She had me change it all, saying there was still significant repair wanting from the malaria, in addition to the havoc of prolonged stress since. I was faithful to her assignments. I rested during the day when Galen was at school and then rose to the best approximation of a normal mom I could manage when he got home.

To be sure, I was alarmed by all of this, but not mortally afraid, and Galen felt that. He knew I knew I would be all right, and for the most part, his world remained intact. My parents and friends drove him wherever he needed to go, and other than the occasional inconvenience of a mom who just couldn't do it (whatever the "it" was), I think he was unaffected. I had enough Social Security to manage for a short while, so I gave up the unrelenting worry about finances and gave all my energy over to a focused sprint to get well. (Which, of course, isn't the way this really works, since real healing is outside an ego-driven timeline of apparent need or convenience. Nonetheless, I got right to it, since I knew it was mine to do, and God was clearly eager to have me listen up.)

I had just begun a contract with a large choir to play a Dvorak program when my eyes forced me off the bench. A friend took over the months of rehearsals while I went into a deep introversion to heal. As the concert date approached, I told the conductor I wanted to play it. Cheating on an assignment of total rest, I had used the intervening months to memorize the music, falling in love with its passionate joy. I couldn't see the notes with any certainty, but memorized, that didn't matter. The shaman working with me said Spirit would cut me a deal for this hubris, but I had to do nine hours of Tai Chi a day for the full week before the concert. I did it. In an act of enormous kindness, the conductor took the risk with me. He, too, wanted to help hold my belief that I would be well again. Once again, music had a ferocious claim on calling me forward—letting me believe in the ineffable goodness of beauty to make things well and whole. On the evenings of the performances, I walked onstage unable to see the faces of the choir surrounding me or the conductor's hands in front of me, but I knew the music and I played, joyous. Every moment of it, every single moment was a gift. And I was so damned lucky to know it.

I realize now, looking back at both episodes of this disease, that two essential relationships framed my determination to be well. One was to the person I loved most, and the second, to a particular piece of music. Both times I was bound by a vitally compelling love, first to a husband and later to a son. This one person mattered absolutely and more than all others. I knew I was needed; I was a partner and a parent and I couldn't let either of them down. In each episode, I was also bound to the deep and guiding sense of music within me that had to be played. I felt it, and knew it was mine to manifest. Two loves—and two relationships: to a beloved and to music. It is impossible to imagine healing without them.

CHAPTER 10

Getting to Now

It is now nearly seven years in. I am finally able to pick up the humbling work of psychotherapy, looking back on what I have done with these years since Gordon died. It's hard work.

I've defended the thesis, gotten the degree, lived with Galen for a short stint in L.A. where he auditioned for film, remodeled our barely built house after a flood, said a tentative yes to someone new who feels certain I am his next partner. Maybe. This, too, is work. For all that anyone wants to enter my life now, they are not the one who went before, and the emptiness in that is astounding. I try the ethically correct efforts at courtesy to forgive someone for not being Gordon, but it's a poor ruse. I can't fake it.

So this writing occurs at the entry of someone new, who helps tend the constant demands of a large piece of rural property, a child in high school needing rides to many rehearsals, a woman who hasn't yet heard back from the world who she senses she is. It's a large assignment for anyone to take on. Maybe I'm not sure yet that I want him to.

Judging all of this, this moment and the years of grieving that have led up to it, is tricky. This writing has felt like being on trial. It has been wrenching to review these last years and see what I think of them, and me. The verdict is still out, for in spite of my efforts to stand self-aware and strong, I am forced to admit that I have been arrested in time since Gordon's death. As I write, I don't know whether to condemn or forgive the person I have been. I have been as pathetic (oh God, notice the judgment) as any other griever I've met, as weak and as lost, and I promised myself I wouldn't be. I was the one with my own hard disease and Africa under my belt, and I knew better than to succumb to self-pity. Well, I succumbed. Maybe it could have been avoided, but maybe not. I suppose the forgiving voice would say that I didn't know how to do it other than the way I did—neither the loving nor the losing.

The therapist parsing this with me now questions whether I will truly love again. The extent of the grief I've born speaks to the obvious observation that Gordon was my soul mate. Maybe, if we get the remarkable good fortune to partner in this way, it is only once in a lifetime. But who knows the rules for any of this living and loving business? Maybe he is right, but maybe my future, like anyone else's, has room for me to want to love again, with even greater depth than before. Maybe in the wanting, there is hope that it may come to pass. If it does, I am blessed. If it does not, I am blessed.

Through all of this, my intent has been to live deeply into each day. To breathe in its gift of time never to be had again, to show up to each encounter, all of me there. I am steered by an urgent need to be fearlessly alive for having lost my love and lost my health. Both have taught me better how to live. No one in their right mind would choose suffering as a means to self-awareness, but for me, at least, the most important things I now understand about life have come this way. I would give anything in the world to have back what I have lost—except for the truths of what these losses have taught me. Perhaps we really can't have it both ways.

But then what kind of a God is that? One who encodes pain with breath? Who encodes pain with boundless love? I suspect that Michael, my trusted companion through all of this, would suggest that the problem is not with God but with me. That true divinity is beyond the maya of suffering and that the real work in a lifetime is to see beyond the illusory veils of attachment. I seem to get more readily tangled in the compelling quality of love's details—the house-holding business of living deeply into meaning through one another. Perhaps in the interweaving that occurs through loving others, I get caught, misunderstanding the necessary ease of also letting go. My heart gets snagged. So here I am, nearly 50 years old, standing at the gate, not sure how many thresholds must be crossed so that there is truly nothing left but love.

CHAPTER 11

Music:
Being Made and Unmade Within It

I believe that I have been carried, both made and unmade, by the sounds in my world—the sounds in my house and my work that have entered my mind and heart. During the early months of grieving, my sense of possibility, of joy or despair, could be determined by the music that happened to be playing on the stereo or the radio at that moment. My heart surfed on these sounds. Usually I was found in my darkest moments, and through the music, led to somewhere lighter by piece's end. In the beginning, it was a magic that I only caught out of the corner of my eye, unaware that I had even been feeling dreadful before I suddenly realized that now, I was not. Gradually I began to notice the contours of these shifts and the magic revealed itself. My mood was being moved by whatever music was in my field.

Since Gordon's death, I have had the radio on all the time, tuned to our local public broadcasting's classical station, and I think that this, as much as anything, has saved my life. I believe I was acutely open to its effects because I had lost my embedded connection with the rest of the world. I had been torn out of my solid, familiar context and reduced to a much simpler, organic awareness that lived within far fewer boundaries. An ego-oriented personality got pried free with Gordon's death and a much less certain, much more connected being swam in my skin. She was the one who knew the gifts of the birds at the feeders, felt the unseen rhythms and energies of a day, the unspoken feelings in a roomful of strangers.

Failing clear differentiation myself, I was attuned to a wholly less differentiated level of consciousness in every setting. I was connected, deeply connected to the feeling world around me. At this level, the organism becomes supremely sensitive to elemental communication. And the most elemental of all is sound. "In the beginning was the Word. . ." Sound organizes form into being, setting vibrations into motion that eventually establish templates for the cellular patterns of creation. Every codified religious tradition in the world pays homage to the awareness that sound is our beginning, the genesis of being. It is the utterly mysterious first impetus for form, the song of existence. In these last shaky years, it has revealed itself as the locus of my remaking. I now know that it was as much the quality of the sound of Michael's voice as what he said when he talked that helped my heart be found in this friendship. I knew his heart by the intonation of his voice.

During the early months, I knew everyone's hearts by their voices. In an instant, I could tell what they were feeling, tuning to the unspoken emotional content of what was being said. This is a deep, intuitive register, communicated at a level before reasoned consciousness. I was attuned to this information because I had been broken down by grief. Edifices of pride and reliable competencies had fallen away. I simply was. This is the first place, the first world of all the world's creation myths, and it is the place of sound, of music, of deep and incautious love. It is where unhesitating compassion occurs between people, fearless love that has no measure of self-gain in it. One experiences great clarity, where all chances to choose love –the essential, small moments of kindness that make the next breath worth drawing—stand out in greater detail. In death, in grieving the loss of a beloved, it is the unbearable tearing, that unmaking of a familiar self, that also makes one whole. And the reweaving is done first in sound.

There is increasing research now being done on the effects of sound on healing and a growing use of music as a self-conscious vehicle of physical transformation. Michael and I have studied music-healing techniques, each of us trying to move what we know from our own experiences into the broader community. I did my graduate work at Reed on various forms of music-medicine. The conservative medical model still finds this new research unnerving and consequently unworthy, but increased well-being and even cure through various applications of music are getting harder to deny. Even if we cannot yet say with certainty why tissue change through sound works (and we can't), nonetheless, it does. Whether we acknowledge it or not, music is a kind of medicine. Other cultures through history have known this, been scrupulous about the uses certain forms of music were put to, and lived within an expectation that music would indeed "change the man."

In recent years, Don Campbell has popularized the idea of a "Mozart Effect," a clever appropriation of the long-held knowledge that music can entrain the body to a slower and more efficient level of functioning so that thinking and learning become easier, more efficient. Taking this a step further, we now know that even without the ability to register the auditory sensations of sound, its vibrations are felt, processed by proprioceptors in the skin that appear to communicate to the central nervous system through a sequence of neuroimmunological exchanges. This is the basis of some of the excitement surrounding the possible applications of the soundbed that Michael and I have used. A large transducer underneath the bed produces sound vibrations that are felt through the skin and that impact the energetic field of the person on the bed. At the same time, this same music, produced in a bi-aural recording, sends differing frequencies through headphones one wears while on the bed. The brain will split the difference between frequencies and jump to an altered state. It has been well established that the most basic body rhythms—those of the heartbeat and breath—are determined by the rhythm and frequency of vibration in the sound fields that surround us. Within these fields, in the constant process of choosing, responding and reforming, we are given the chance to become anew; at some extremely fundamental level to choose again who we are to be.

I believe that sound served as the organic substrate of our healing. Music supported the deepest level of repair that Michael and I were experiencing. In our extreme vulnerability, we began to notice the profound effects sounds had upon us, including the sounds of one another's voices. We were embraced by sound, held safe in our self-consciously chosen music in essential and mysterious ways, remade by it. As musicians, we both now feel the obligation to admit to this terrible importance music and sound play in our lives, that music plays in all of our lives, whether we have had experiences that have allowed us to become acutely aware of it or not. Sound, music, matter. It is the deepest part of what makes us who we are. It is what sings love into being. It is how three of us have survived.

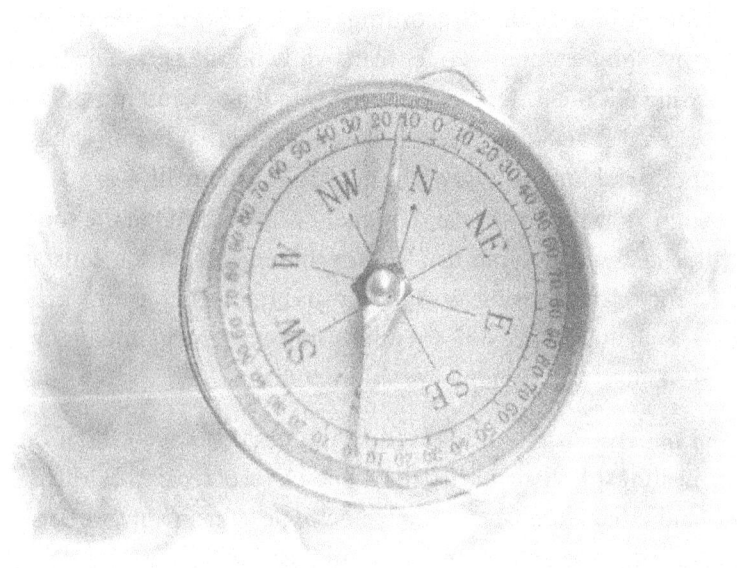

SECTION THREE

A Conversation
Where We Are Today

Good-night! good-night! as we so oft have said
Beneath this roof at midnight, in the days
That are no more, and shall no more return.
Thou hast but taken up thy lamp and gone to bed;
I stay a little longer, as one stays
To cover up the embers that still burn.

— Henry Wadsworth Longfellow —

2000

2011

Our Continuing Journey
June 2011

Hsü / Waiting (Nourishment)

How does it feel now, 16 years later, as we come together again to look back?

Michael: Like most things, this traumatic episode 16 years ago feels like a dream to me. It sounded an alarm, difficult to ignore or deny, that forced my hand: I had to change who I was and what I was becoming.

Not long ago, I read about these large sheets of ice that razed hundreds of square miles of earth during the last ice age. The ice flows crushed all the rocks and hills in their path, mineralizing the earth in such a way as to make the ground fertile for plants and trees to flourish. There was no other way that plant life could have taken root so successfully. I was the rock and she was the glacial mass.

Similarly, Mount Vesuvius' eruptions have rendered the area around Pompeii among the most prized growing regions in the world. I'm not trying to trivialize a vastly important and dramatic event in my life or in yours, but I'm trying to open it up to a broader perspective. And in the grandest of cosmologies, I think life's axiom is simply that the new can only emerge from the recently destroyed.

The same, I suppose, could be said for all natural disasters. What seems, from our puny human perspective, to be devastating and cruel is just the way it all happens. Some things "just happen." Maya's sudden and untimely death happened to me, and the glacial raze of her sudden departure incited growth in me that I can't deny. Did I accept the challenge to grow, as seeds sprout and stretch toward their beloved sun above, reveling in the most fantastic gift of all: new life? I have no idea. A hole was left and, by default or design, I filled it with something else. I dealt, as best I could, with the anguish and fractured spirit. But am I a better person? A deeper, more thoughtful person? I have no idea. But I learned in a way that nothing else could have made me learn. And I think I have actually grown in a way that no other singular event could have made me grow. And now, 16 years later, I think the sprouts in the razed landscape of my being have begun to bear something new and worthwhile. Time is the Revealer; time is the Healer.

Jennifer: "Some things just happen." Boy, do I have trouble with that! I don't feel like the love between Gordon and me just happened. We hoed, weeded, watered, fertilized it. We tended that garden and it flourished. Granted, our meeting was a gift, but we made the efforts to grow. Maybe, in part, that's why the thievery of his death felt so much like betrayal.

"Razed." Oh Lord, yes. Part of a cycle to "make the ground fertile?" I guess. You're feeling time as the sun's gift that brings new seeds to life in you. I'm feeling the weariness of having been ground to rubble. Do I feel receptive, new? Nope, I feel old. And I wonder, could I ever love and hurt this much again? Probably not. I suspect I have neither the courage nor the sinew to survive such vulnerability again.

I read what we wrote 16 years ago and feel grateful for our stamina, but the stories are hard, Michael. Grinding to grist is great for granite but tough on the heart. I was wondering, hoping that there would be some lesson learned, some achieved wisdom from our introspection, but I become the new widow as I read what I wrote right after Gordon's death. Maybe that is one of the big things about death: time loses its linear quality. Having ridden through the early days of widowhood, I know that straight-forward progress is a fiction.

I can't argue with your if-then equation of "destruction before creation," but my experience of the hard math of maturity feels muddled into more of a simultaneity. I seem to be as readily tripped by days of surprising weariness as I do by gifts of blessed strength, and often feel no wiser for the increasing grey hair. My experience is more kindred to the snake of time eating its tail. It's all going on, but I'm not sure, really, where I am in it, even though I keep trying for certainty. Time is exquisitely slippery.

Beyond trying to figure out if I might have achieved some new and worthy insight in this reckoning with death, I do know that a singular love that seeks the same depth I shared with Gordon is likely impossible. This is my limit, not that of the beloved before me. But in its place (well, maybe not a substitution—who knows what calls forth different types of love?), I seem to love much more broadly than before. At this point in my life, I feel obligated to show up as fully as I am able, to attend to the person in front of me. No matter the circumstance, I am aware that this moment is all there is, and I am called to love the best I can.

Perhaps a wider eye to those before me is a gift of suffering through widowhood? Maybe; losses and gains.

Lin / Approach

Where are we with our losses?

Michael: I find that I'm losing every day. I'm losing skin cells as they are sloughing off my body. I'm losing family. I've lost friends to cancer. I'm losing time. Man, am I losing time. I'm trying to make peace with the whole notion of time because the human concept of the linear passage of time is a bully. And it's a straight-jacket on my spirit. Nonetheless, I see the ravages of its linearity in the decreasing elasticity of my muscles and tendons. The once supple, agile body machine is showing signs of wear. At the very least, it's asking to be treated with more attention and kindliness. Perhaps that, more than anything, has caused me to refocus on "time theft" and "time left." And why not spend it while the body machine is still cooperating, traveling, discovering, throwing myself into new situations, countries, cultures? Like Maya, without consideration, when she shed her clothes and jumped with a wild little girl abandon into the ice cold Oregon spring ocean.

So, before losing too much buoyancy, I want to celebrate this life. And stare into the gaping maw of death's relentless appearance on the horizon and declare that I'm going to have a whole lot of fun. I'm going to love a whole lot more. I'm going to lighten the load of my possessions and the meaningless time-sucks on the internet, and laugh in the face of death's inevitability. I'm going to focus on the eternal rather than the linear concept of time. I'm going to embrace loss as something that simply happens in nature.

Jennifer: Oh Michael, see where we are? You're rocketing forward into opportunity and I remain pretty blasted bewildered. How could our losses have marked us so differently? I am aging into a reckoned disappointment with missed adventure, with damnable physical limits, with wondering how to live out this last bit in order to die well. Now, 16 years later, I realize I am desperate to reclaim a passionate life, one that is not written in the syntax of survival. I want this before I die. I have worked hard these last 16 years. It's what I know how to do. I had to. My losses? Play. I lost play. I lost trust that if I didn't worry about it, it still might turn out OK. I lost risk. I lost solitude—deep, creative solitude. I have soldiered these past 16 years, and I need a furlough.

Wu Wang / Innocence (The Unexpected)

How have we changed since writing our stories ten years ago?

Michael: I feel far less certain about things than I did 10 years ago. I felt I'd come out on the other side of a long courtship with grief. Now I feel that little losses are washing over me constantly. I know considerably less, and I feel lighter because of it. I guess it doesn't hurt that I have just reallocated everything I own to other people and Goodwill.

Lightness is what I'm focusing on now. And that has been the gift of the years spent in healing the loss of my wife. As I read what I wrote 10 years ago, I feel the need to comfort the person who wrote those words, like I want to comfort a hurting child. I feel my pain again, but it's receded into manageability, far off in the distance. The man who wrote these words is like another person—a person for whom I have so much compassion.

I still cry when I think of Maya. It'll hit me out of nowhere. I'll remember our playfulness and muse over how much I miss her. She still appears in my dreams, and I see her in other people's faces. Am I different than I was a decade ago? Definitely. Far less certain. I actually know, and assume, far less.

Jennifer: "Far less certain." Absolutely. I'm much more generous toward what I don't know about another person, or about life. I don't sweat the small stuff anymore. I can't get excited about petty complaints—I simply don't have the energy for it. This can frustrate the hell out of the folks I'm with, but I can't even want to help it. I've learned to abide in the field of excitement around me without feeling obligated to enter it.

Another difference from the woman of 10 years ago is that I am far less hopeful about my life coming around right, i.e., The Happy Life. The one I remember from Before. Rather, this is it: this day. All I have is my attitude toward it, toward the work and the people in it, toward the possibility for change. I seem resolved to a certain isness of matters as they present themselves. I have lost a ready faith in their ability to transform toward joy. Maybe over these years, I've lost contact with magic.

So, curiously, you write of feeling lighter, and I am feeling more stolid. That is not the same as grounded. Stolid implies resigned. Even though I hate to admit it, the bound muscles of my back give truth to a decade of making do. I have failed at finding a healthy measure of abandon and delight. I have forgotten how to goof off.

K'un / The Receptive

Are we any more certain of love and life than we were? What remains baffling, and what seems clear and probably true?

Michael: Again, I seem far less clear now than I did then. I'm now thinking that absolutely everything that happens is a mystery, a mystery that requires my surrender. And the more I surrender, the easier I am able to live with myself. But surrendering is a practice all by itself: one of my biggest lessons, one of my biggest challenges. It sits patiently at my doorstep like the visitor who won't go away. One of the biggest mysteries in my life has been Maya's sudden death. Why her? Why me? Why death? What is death? It's all a mystery.

I had a dream last night, and saw the world in which all my dreams play out. All the dreams were played on the one singular stage: the stage set of my experience, my story. All the props on the stage were ones I'd used thousands of times in other dreams. Essentially, the stage was the same in EVERY dream, but with a slight re-dressing. I regarded this realization, still within the dream, as a revelation, a "wow." But I was also aware in the dream that there are many other realities, that my stage was minuscule compared to the vastness of life's story, that mine was only a reality I'd written for myself, that I could blow it open to something inconceivably and mysteriously larger.

Jennifer: I want that dream. I know it's self-created, this whole landscape of my life. I am hamstrung by habit so I keep holding this one form in place. Loving within it, to be sure, but keeping it small, maybe because I don't ever want to feel that lonely again. EVER. So I remain within a context of familiarity and suffocate in daily doses of barely managed panic. Probably a shitty compromise now that I write it, but I have been unable to call in help to change the fundamental habit of me, in spite of YEARS of diligent therapy. It is no doubt an excellent thing that I am returning to a meditation practice. Some of the ballast may fall away. I certainly hope so. I want that larger stage that you're on, Michael. The one that isn't framed by fear.

So, what do I feel certain about? Love is all that matters. All the time. It's the whole deal. It's not just an outside job. It's the inside one that's hardest. Loving the person whose history is yours. REALLY loving her. Listening, tending well to her heart's voice. But then not just listening, but care-taking this truth as it is given. Responding in ways that let me know I've been listening to myself, my deeper self.

But you know what? To hear this voice, there has to be some trustworthy quiet. Otherwise the yammering demands of the world will drown it out. And this precious quiet, I realize, I have subtracted from a life deafened by the whir of surviving.

If I just open my eyes, damn it, I can't help but notice that the fight is over. I have a son who is on his own trajectory as an artist, I have work and community I value and bills I am lucky enough to be able to pay. The fact of the matter is that the 43-year-old widow got the essential care-taking stuff done, the survival stuff. Maybe the suffocation is confusion about where I am in time. The pregnant novelty of "now" has been buried in "then" and I have remained with an embattled warrior's heart, blind to the truth that that struggle is finished. It's time to listen anew to this good old beating heart of mine. It's been 16 years. Wow, how is that possible?

Kuan / Contemplation (View)

Did gender have anything to do with how we grieved?

Michael: As we mature as men and women, I would think that we'd become less and less identified with our gender and more identified with our soul natures. Do our defining male and female traits recede in their outward appearance and importance as we mature? Let's face it—strip away the personality and social contrivance, and you're left with a person that can only love a person that only knows love.

But...summarizing here, and this is what I feel makes our combined voices so full of color and dimension: You were married for 17 years and you were both raising a child. Maya and I were married for three months and, while we didn't have a child, intended to.

Given the different natures of our relationships, one would think we'd have different perspectives on how grief is observed. You relied heavily on the support of friends and family and, for whatever reason, I did not. You deepened your relationship with your faith; I did not. And wouldn't you, as a woman, ascribe a different value to your feelings than a man would?

But knowing you, and based on what we've both experienced through this, I think grieving has a lot more to do with who the person is and how they deal with change and adversity, than it has to do with gender. Though our stages were set very differently, our experience of the loss was similar. Particularly in the way in which we sought to heal ourselves: through music.

So let me ask you: *how do you feel your grief experience was different from mine?*

Jennifer: OK, my dear, here goes. I was completely caught up with surviving and feeling my way into connection with Gordon's ongoingness, wherever that might be in time and space. Stabbing tree roots into the earth was an imperative and urgent claim, as was the music and trying to love and care for my son. I didn't get terribly caught up in trying to understand the point of all this for me; I was more thickly tied to trying to find purchase in the present moment, however it presented itself. But I sense that yours has been a more careful, intellectual journey, trying to find meaning for yourself in this and God's intent for all the players.

Although I reconnoitered a possibly worthy, if unfathomable point in this pain for Galen and me, flirting with the hope of ultimate meaning was a far step from taking God head-on as a TEACHER in all this. I merely knew that considering suicide was a viscerally repugnant thought, so I tried not to. Other than hoping for a holy compass to lead me to Gordon, the role of the divine in this remains a mystery to me. I may have had a more organic process, in the sense of being held by the world in essential, inextricably entangled ways. Your trajectory seems more reasoned, linear, aimed at self-understanding and transformation. My efforts were in the service of muddling through—survival.

Michael: I see a good deal of similarity in our respective experiences. We were faced with the same dilemma: how can I reconstruct a life that makes sense in present time given that my limbs are scattered all around me? The period of grieving (as if it ever really stops) was perhaps marked more by questions than anything else, and I'd venture that your questions were much like my mine:

How can I communicate with her?

Why do I have no desire to be with others who have little or no understanding for this uniquely altered state?

Who's to say what's real anymore?

How can I go on living in the same way, particularly with no road map?

I would say that, for your part, there might have been more of a perilous divide between your responsibility as a mother and the more vague responsibility of simply keeping your head above water. While survival was your response to the unthinkable, my response was – since I felt I had no one to live for but myself – do I choose life, and if so, why? And what will it look like?

Jennifer: You're right. I think my response to Gordon's death was framed very much by my sense of obligation to those nearest—my son and absent husband. I mustered strength on behalf of others, delaying the more terrifying encounter with my own redefinition. I am only now facing the work of your question, "Do I choose life, and if so, what will it look like?" What will MY life look like? I haven't known how to ask, let alone answer this essential, selfish, life-affirming question. In this, I think you've led. It was immediately in front of you, while I had other demands that allowed it to remain at a farther remove.

I think we've both asked, "What does this death mean? What does any of it mean?" But I think you may have come closer to an answer. You've wrestled God into an easy-gaited compassion, while I've still got God walking with a powerfully disturbing limp. At the deepest level I'm not sure what's afoot in being alive or how I am to answer to it. I am always a little or a lot afraid. ALWAYS. But it does boil down to God, doesn't it? That's what these losses and gains have been about. I'm still steering clumsily, but I see you navigate, oh so deliberately, toward an unballasted loftiness, an airborne reach for divinity.

Do you really think the differences have only to do with my needing to parent through this? Might not the freedom to engage the question, "what do I want to make of my life?" come more readily to a man? Or at least to a man who hadn't been the homemaking/tending partner in a long-term relationship? Even though I carried a professional identity, my stronger identity was as the luckiest woman in the world to be THIS man's wife. Stepping from that into, "It's your oyster now baby, shuck it and get the pearl of a new life," is a long distance to travel. My isness was imbedded into my relationship with Gordon.

Michael: "Unballasted loftiness." Jen, you crack me up. In your tireless generosity of spirit, you've used the word "loftiness" instead of "madness." Given that I've never been married, save the brief flight with Maya, my entire life could easily be characterized as unballasted madness. Women have been a harbor of sanity for me, and my unballasted madness often took consolation in that harbor. Women have felt like the only real refuge. The doppelganger here is that while women seem to have more of a fluidity and essential ease as they do life, there is also a somewhat frightening attendant unpredictability that can cause a man to tremble more in a woman's presence than looking down the barrel of a gun. So while this being careens for the harbor, the harbor itself can be like "the fickle moon, the inconstant moon, that monthly changes in her circle orb".

The question that begs for an answer now is: Will I ever be able to love again and give myself without reserve to a partnership that may be whisked away in the blink of a fateful eye?

Clearly, it's all just up to me. Being as good and as informed a person as I can be. And that's about it.

I went through the grieving process like a lost boy with an obsessive penchant for making mathematical sense out of disorder. When I think of the disarray my life was in after losing Maya, the image that comes to mind is Darth Vader hurtling through space at the end of one of the Star Wars movies.... "to be continued..."

Jennifer: Here's what I think. At some point, all of us have to reckon with pain. We are born bruised into being. Somewhere along the way, it becomes easier to lift bewildering, inexplicable pain outside ourselves, seeking relief from the effort of holding too complex a truth. We can make enemies across borders, religions, color, sex—the permutations on unconscious efforts to remove the distress of not knowing a source for this a priori hurt are endless. Our hearts can't bear so capricious and difficult a God.

So, did gender make a difference for us in grieving? I think so. I have thrown myself into efforts at obedience as an answer to the pain of simply being alive. I am driven by heartache—a gut panic at terrible disorder in the world, and the certainty that there is a wrong that must be righted. I am haunted by a screaming intuition that our misery surely must be influenced by some effort I can make that will help reweave us, healing the world whole and right. Pain free. It is this call to action, the heroism of the effort, that keeps me from drowning in despair. My heart believes in the battle. If I felt unable to enter the pain of being, of life, without some ability to shift it, the cruelty of another dawn would be unbearable. My way of managing the complexity of suffering has been to enter it; no other choice seems available to me. But in the entering, there is the constant undercurrent belief that I am being watched, judged, and that it is entirely possible to fail. I live with an Old Testament God in my heart, because for the most part, I have been afraid to live without one at all.

Given this, Gordon's death has been the grand reenactment of these core fears. I have done most of what's been achieved in these last years out of fear. I have wanted to prove to my dead husband that I loved him THIS much, to the collective community that I have tried THIS honorably, to my hovering God that I have been THIS confounded in an effort to do things right. Certainly that's all good, isn't it? And yet threaded through it all is the guiding belief that there is someone to whom I must prove my worth, that I must please, and who will determine my right to be. I haven't had the means or the courage to allow the possibility that I might be deeply, truly, terribly on my own. And that, Michael, is a bedrock uncertainty that I believe many women my age share.

The God of our times has been primarily a masculine imagination, and we have until recent time called this uncertainty "He." I have been trying to answer to, understand, and forgive the utterly bewildering mean-spiritedness of this "He" all my life. I have been making frantic efforts at owning my life, my singular expression of isness, from somewhere at the feet of his throne. As a woman, I have never had the illusion of sharing the dais with this God. He's a man; I am not. Much of what I have done and felt in the course of grieving Gordon's death has been done out of confusion about who I am, and who God is or is not. I have made efforts to be obedient to a perceived sense of overriding order in a universe that has fallen under the arm of a God whose form is too small and who looks nothing like me. I have not only been lost as a wife in this; I have been lost as a woman.

I don't think that obedience, and existential definition, have been so thoroughly up for grabs for you. I suspect that if they have not, it is because you enjoy the small comfort, real or no, of being a man inheriting the cultural ascription of a male form and language to address the most terrifying power of all. If we call this unknowing that holds the comings and goings of life in its embrace "He," there is no greater accumulation of power in the universe. You get to identify with the untouchable male manna of divinity; I do not. I merely sit at his feet, mighty damned confused.

Michael: If your God has been the punitive male sort, my inspiration has always been a woman. Without a woman, my life feels devoid of warmth, love or understanding.

Haven't we both, in ways that feel finally understandable, committed the same human error? Haven't we projected romanticized versions of what love is onto someone outside ourselves? And when our beloved is ripped from our lives, are we not then faced with the imperative to sort it all out…all over again?

Was this a cruel lesson, a cruel joke? Or was it just something that happened to cause us to ask why? Why do I feel incomplete? Why do I feel not enough? Why do I feel alone? Why do I feel that I've got to get it "right?" Why am I plagued with the nagging awareness of my imperfection?

These are the questions our beloveds might well ask of us. We are asked, with all the tenderness that the universe can muster, to simply look at the questions.

For as certainly as our spouses loved us, we are loved, with or without them in our lives. For as certainly as Maya gave me emotional support and Gordon gave you a sense of rightness in the world you made for yourselves, the mirrors they hold up to us reside deep in our own knowing. What an incredibly great way to return the blessing of their love for us: to show them that their love, support, understanding and compassion is mirrored back to us when we are in the presence of virtually anyone or anything. Just as I felt Maya's love for me when I'd look in your eyes and just as I heard her sweet voice through your voice. Just as I felt her heart pounding against my chest as we'd hug one another in greeting.

How very propitious that we should meet weeks after our spouses' spirits flew. They live alright. They live and it's all right. You helped keep Maya alive for me just by being there. You reflected her patience and compassion.

Jennifer: Okey-doke, Mr. Mish. You got me. I am in tears. "To show them that their love, support, understanding and compassion is mirrored back to us when we are in the presence of virtually anything." Virtually anything. VIRTUALLY ANYTHING. That's it. That's all there is. And, of course, you and I are mirrors for each other's gifts of love. I guess we did do it differently AND we did it together, and it is unimaginable otherwise. Having you, this friendship, Michael, has been at the heart of the answer to my pain. Maybe that's the larger truth—you, Gordon, Galen, my friends and family, the Methodist Church community, the Jewish community, the audiences who've loved me, the audiences who've hated me—they have all held the weave. Even in the awfulest absence, love came. Love was. Love is. Does that mean that I, too, am fundamentally lovable as well? But if I don't have to prove, achieve, or save anything or anyone, where is honor? Does God care whether I feel compelled to these efforts?

Somehow, I think so, but maybe with a compassion so immense that I simply cannot breathe it in. I sense that. Oh God, I am starting over. Really, truly starting over again: wrestling with being in a life and the enormity of its miracle, not the least being the wonder of our having met one another.

"Being deeply loved by someone gives you strength, while loving someone deeply gives you courage."

— Lao Tzu —

EPILOGUE

Final Reflections
Somewhere This Side of Eternity

We shall not cease from exploration.
And the end of all our exploring
Will be to arrive at where we started
And know the place for the first time.

— T. S. Eliot —

Time
September 2011

Jennifer: Michael, I had 17 years bucketing through adventures with a man I admired and loved. We had a wonder child the doctors told me I shouldn't, who lit up our lives. Threaded through it, until the very end, we had shared our breath in making music together. The bonding was deep. We were wrapped in an eternity of our own making, a story of overcoming and of joy. Time had written a singular signature for us, where opportunity's horizon remained flexible and open. It wasn't until Gordon's cancer that the door slammed shut. Although you may well have basked in a kindred spaciousness, enjoying the expansive hopes of a future, you lost the gifts of a shared history. You weren't offered the years of "we" that had to be reconciled, the loomed lives that became unraveled in death. We had years of woodchopping our relationship; soul-sweating sessions of breaking our fears down small enough that we had a shot at intimacy. You were just starting. It is my sense that in the grieving you interrogated your soul to write a history you weren't given. That you intended to travel an arc you intuited— and that you were going to claim whatever you could of love's blistering lessons in relationship, even if your partner was silent. I believe that you were determined not to shortchange

Maya or yourself. So—you made a heroic effort to live a relationship history of your own making, in a private world of grief.

Time dealt us different hands. I was given a history and you made yours.

I think that difference has shaped us, not only in the initial reckoning, but in these years after as well. I lost who I was. You lost who you might have become.

My timelessness was in the dailyness of relationship. I have had to search like mad to find it in solitude. You didn't have a chance to deepen the daily hum with Maya. You were just starting your duet—and I think because of it, you have found your way back to a solo line with a readier facility than I.

Michael: Jennifer, I was in such a good place when Maya and I met. I was in step with the rhythm of my life. Things were going swimmingly. When my life was finally making sense to me, I felt rewarded in meeting Maya and jilted by the heavens when she was ripped from me. I'd personified fate, latching onto a God who doled out "good" and "bad" circumstances. GOOD: I was on the receiving end of this wonderful gift. BAD: it was suddenly and sickeningly denied me. I must tell you that I feel differently about this now. God didn't do anything to me. I wasn't rewarded and I wasn't scolded. This experience happened in my life and I had these reactions to it. If there was a learning in it, so much the better. If there wasn't a learning in it, it would have been a damnable waste of time and energy. But it wasn't a waste of time and energy. I learned a lot.

Being on the receiving end of the sting of loss, my mind went to all kinds of victim places. "I've been a basically bad person, so this happened to me." At the time, it was the only way my brain made sense of the unfairness of it.

For a time, Jennifer, I imagined life continuing with her. Like she was this silent witness always with me. Our life was carrying on as if nothing had happened. Her presence, though wispy and lacking in her former fire, was a presence that comforted me. It was the only way my mind would allow for the inexplicable and sudden absence in my life. My desperation created a shadowy facsimile of the woman.

I now see that to have acted as I did reveals my store of endless grief, always there. Grief that is beyond my memory and awareness. And, that this particular grief, losing Maya, was a bittersweet invitation to explore something really, really magnificent.

In our case, it brought you and me together, Jennifer, to look at just how useful, wondrous and loving a friendship can be. I will be grateful beyond time and measure for the ways you were there for me. Through you I learned that madness, angst, macabre imaginings, and deep sorrow all have a rightness about them. At a time when I felt very, very wrong, you helped me to feel right again. Feeling spectacularly un-human and quite alone, I learned what an abiding friendship can do to re-seat the being into a human and shared experience. That there can be nothing more important than friendship in this life.

In my case, grief shattered illusions I had about myself. And the illusions about myself were keeping me from living more fully. I can no longer make the little concessions that most of us feel we must make in order to be socially acceptable. My heart won't let me. I can no longer pretend I'm someone I'm not. My heart won't allow it.

Jennifer, I admire the richness of what you created with Gordon. I envy the time you had. You had seasons with Gordon. Seasons! You had time to settle into a marriage and watch how your love was able to incorporate and manage the day-to-day. This remains something tantalizing and sublime to me: to experience love's high flight gently floating to the ground to intermingle with the earthbound ordinariness of washing dishes and taking out the garbage. I would've loved to have settled into that. And though I'm sure you had your moments of relationship unsteadiness, I know you had that great, great knowing that when you reached over in the middle of the night, he was there. He was breathing, or snoring or fidgeting. But, he was there.

I've moved into an open place of readiness for the next relationship adventure. I look forward to reaching over and gently nudging her as she snores; to looking down at the floor when we disagree; to picking her up at the dentist's office after anesthesia. To wiping away the stray hair that manages to fall in front of her eyes. To all the ordinary things that most couples alternately enjoy and dislike. I know that it is there and it waits for me. But I will bring so very much more to it this time around. I'll bring a full heart and a readiness to experience what is to come without feeling like I'm being rewarded or chastised by a fickle God. I'll take the good with the bad, knowing that good and bad are only human qualities. That life is what life is. And life, for me anyway, is good.

Jennifer: Grief shattered the illusion of social courtesy for you. The belief that we need to behave according to the cultural formulas our parents worked so hard to entrust to us. Because, what if we didn't? Exactly. What if we didn't????

Freedom. Lonely and sublime.

One of Maya's great gifts to you was to bust open your agreement to the collective script. You can't pretend to feel less than you do, know less than you do, care less than you do, or act as if ignoring what is true won't matter. It does, and you know it. But I think, Michael, in this razor-edged integrity, you may have scant company. In dating, the negotiations of courtship seem to involve a million small surrenders that easily swerve off into subtle dishonesties—dinky soul cheats that allow the game to go on. I don't imagine there are many who have the courage to really show up, Michael, and continue to risk it all, knowing that if they don't, they have nothing. How many of us know that? For as much as you are willing to invest the whole of yourself in loving a new partner, she will need to be someone of equal courage. The ground for beginning needs to be even and forgiving, so you can feel the easy rhythm of one another's walk before you encounter the boulders you must inevitably scramble. I want that for you. I want that for me. Because you know what? Neither of us is very good at lying anymore.

I think the timelessness that we've talked about exists not only in the hope for what can arise in an intimate relationship built on deep courage and integrity, but also in the awareness that ALL relationships are soul matters. Our friendship taught me that. From some-terrifying-where in outer space, I came home in this relationship with you because you made room for utter, mucky honesty. We healed in that ruthless, forgiving vessel of one another's love, and then went into the world again, hopeful and odd.

If I look back at our passage and try to enfold it in a larger snapshot of my life, I see that we've ended up at the same milepost. The whole blasted deal has been about surrender for me. Seeing and appreciating the wonder of the clumsy efforts, the failed attempts, and unnoticed success of the ordinary. Slicing off the arrogance of wishing the world were what it isn't, and forgiving and loving it for what it is. Recognizing that trying to measure a life as good and bad is our poor feeble effort at understanding something wildly beyond our knowing. Or, in your words, that life is what life is. And that for you and for me, Michael, it is good.

Epilogue

*Eternity is really long,
especially near the end.*

— Woody Allen —